THE PARTY
of the
FIRST PART

THE PARTY
of the
FIRST PART

THE CURIOUS WORLD
OF LEGALESE

ADAM FREEDMAN

HENRY HOLT AND COMPANY
NEW YORK

HENRY HOLT AND COMPANY, LLC
PUBLISHERS SINCE 1866
175 FIFTH AVENUE
NEW YORK, NEW YORK 10010
WWW.HENRYHOLT.COM

HENRY HOLT® AND ® ARE REGISTERED TRADEMARKS OF HENRY HOLT AND
COMPANY, LLC.

DISTRIBUTED IN CANADA BY H. B. FENN AND COMPANY LTD.

LIBRARY OF CONGRESS CATALOGING-IN-PUBLICATION DATA

FREEDMAN, ADAM.
   THE PARTY OF THE FIRST PART : THE CURIOUS WORLD OF LEGALESE / ADAM
FREEDMAN. — 1ST ED.
      P. CM.
   INCLUDES BIBLIOGRAPHICAL REFERENCES AND INDEX.
   ISBN-13: 978-0-8050-8223-4
   ISBN-10: 0-8050-8223-9
   1. LAW—UNITED STATES—ANECDOTES.   2. LAW—UNITED STATES—HUMOR.
3. LAW—UNITED STATES—LANGUAGE.   4. ENGLISH LANGUAGE—UNITED
STATES—RHETORIC.   I. TITLE.
   KF184.F74 2007
   349.7301'4—DC22
                                                    2007004480

HENRY HOLT BOOKS ARE AVAILABLE FOR SPECIAL PROMOTIONS AND PREMIUMS.
FOR DETAILS CONTACT: DIRECTOR, SPECIAL MARKETS.

FIRST EDITION 2007

DESIGNED BY MERYL SUSSMAN LEVAVI

PRINTED IN THE UNITED STATES OF AMERICA

10   9   8   7   6   5   4   3   2   1

To Kathleen

CONTENTS

THE PARTY
of the
FIRST PART

1

THE GLORY OF

LEGALESE

"*Incorporeal*" *means "without a body."*
However, when a company is "incorporated"
it is given a body.

— CENTRE FOR PLAIN LEGAL LANGUAGE, 1995

At 2:30 A.M. on March 22, 1997, a convicted felon named Anthony Dye was racing his Corvette through the streets of Elkhart, Indiana. The police were in hot pursuit. Dye pulled into his mother's driveway, got out of the car, and made a run for it. When the police caught up with him, Dye took a semiautomatic pistol from his waistband and opened fire. At that critical moment, a valiant police dog named Frei leapt into action, fastened onto Dye's leg, and, as it were, took a bite out of crime. Dye was arrested.

Having been injured in the course of his arrest, Dye did what any red-blooded American would do. He brought a lawsuit—against Frei the police dog. Dye argued that dogs are "persons" who can be sued, at least when they work for the police. Dye fought his way to the second highest court in the land, the United States Court of Appeals, which dismissed his claim.

Dye's theory that a dog is a person is not as far-fetched as you might think. In fact, he wasn't even the first person to sue a police dog. And some very respectable lawyers have argued that the legal definition of person ought to be expanded, at least to include other primates. Laurence Tribe, Harvard's leading constitutional scholar, has maintained for years that chimpanzees should be considered persons under the Constitution.

That the country's best legal minds can be consumed with questions about whether the word "person" includes dogs or chimpanzees tells us a lot about lawyers. But it also tells us something about the *language* of the law. Nothing in the realm of legalese is quite what it seems.

Consider the fact that Congress once passed legislation declaring that "September 16, 1940 means June 27, 1950." In New Zealand, the law says that a "day" means a period of seventy-two hours, while an Australian statute defines "citrus fruit" to include eggs. To American lawyers, a twenty-year-old document is "ancient," while a seventeen-year-old person is an "infant." At one time or another, the law has defined "dead person" to include nuns, "daughter" to include son, and "cow" to include horse; it has even declared white to be black.

At times, legalese appears to be almost willfully perverse. Standard legal agreements, for example, typically contain some version of the following clause:

> The masculine shall include the feminine, the singular shall include the plural, and the present tense shall include the past and future tenses.

In other words, the law sees absolutely no difference between "the boy becomes a man" and "girls will be girls."

Well, then. All this would be of purely academic interest if it weren't for the fact that legal documents are part of the basic infrastructure of life. Isn't it odd that the most important events in our lives require slogging through language that almost nobody understands?

Think about it: getting married or divorced, buying or renting property, investing a nest egg, making a will, serving on a jury, declaring bankruptcy, taking out insurance, borrowing money, getting sued, undergoing surgery— each one of these transactions involves lengthy documents that we are expected to sign, usually without having had sufficient time to read them. Indeed, a person who insists on reading everything that he signs is regarded as a crank of the first order.

And yet, if you ask an educated person, he will often tell you, in self-satisfied tones, that he would never sign a document that he hadn't read. "Wouldn't dream of it," he'll say, perhaps tugging at his bow tie and straightening his horn-rimmed glasses, "I won't agree to anything unless I have time to read it over."

Not to put too fine a point on it, but I don't believe this hypothetical educated person. Does he actually read every car rental contract in full? Does he pore over every agreement sent to him by a credit card company, and the warranty on every product that he buys? Does he read every software licensing agreement before clicking "I agree"? If the answer to all of these is "yes," then I dare say he also lines his hat with aluminum foil.

Consider the case of Justin Noe, a British motorist who was pulled over by the police in 1999 and asked to submit to a Breathalyzer test. He agreed, but on the condition that he first be allowed to consult the Police and Criminal Evidence Act; that is, the very law that explains a citizen's rights when taking Breathalyzer tests. A court later decided that Noe's request was so patently unreasonable as to constitute a refusal to submit to the test, the implication being that he was probably drunk. Clearly, anybody who asks to read a statute must be intoxicated.

When nonlawyers do manage to read legal documents, they typically end up more confused than they were before they started. Any language in which **libel** can mean either a disparaging remark or a lawsuit against a ship is obviously a disaster waiting to happen. In legalese, when you **execute** an agreement, you bring it into existence; but when you execute a person, you do just the opposite. A layman is often surprised to learn that only land and buildings count as **real property**, as though things like cars and furniture were somehow *un*real property. Actually, the "real" in real property comes from the French word for "royal," because all land used to be held by the king. There, doesn't that make you feel better?

The double and triple meanings of legal language account for many of the odd newspaper headlines that make the rounds on the Internet—"Man struck by lightning faces battery charge," for example. Or "Juvenile court to try shooting defendant." Now *there's* an idea.

MIND THE GAP

In 2001, the *Economist* magazine reported on a "worrying gap" between the language of the public and that of the legal profession. That gap grows wider every day, as legal English staunchly resists the changes rippling through everyday English. On the bright side, this means that the law is less susceptible to silly fads—lawyers don't write things like "gr8—cu l8r!"—but it also means that the law is less and less accessible to each new generation.

Legalese could even evolve into a foreign language in the not-too-distant future. Already, many linguists refer to the language of law as a "sublanguage," meaning that it's more than just a collection of jargon, but also has its own specialized rules of grammar and syntax. How many ordinary English speakers understand the common mortgage term that asks you to promise that you are "lawfully **seised** of the estate to be conveyed"? Or the promissory note that makes you waive your right to "**interpose any counter-claim**"? Sublanguage indeed.

The fact that legalese is drifting away from everyday language is especially sad since the story of legal English is, in many ways, the story of the English language itself. There are statutes recorded in English going back to the Laws of Ine, the Anglo-Saxon king of Wessex, in the late seventh century A.D. Ine's laws were admirably straightforward. For example:

If anyone steals so that his wife and children do not know, let him pay sixty shillings fine. If he should steal with the knowledge of his family, then they should all go into slavery.

6 What could be clearer? For centuries, legal language played a decisive role in the development of English. The very first dictionary printed in England (in 1523) was a law dictionary written by John Rastell, a true Renaissance man who at various times was a playwright, theatrical producer, printer, translator, failed explorer, and, of course, lawyer. The first English-language dictionary to include word etymologies was also a law dictionary, Thomas Blount's 1670 *Nomo-Lexikon*.

In 1607, lawyer John Cowell came out with a massive dictionary called *The Interpreter*. The book was intended as a legal glossary, but such was Cowell's enthusiasm for words that he could not help veering off topic, defining such nonlegal words as cinnamon, condor, fodder, and pier, not to mention polein (the pointy tip of a boot) and senie (a medicinal herb).

One of the great pleasures of perusing old law dictionaries is the glimpse we get of a vanished society. In Cowell's book we see the sturdy **shyreeve**, the "shire reeve," a
local constable, whose title would eventually morph into
sheriff. There are **markets** and **staples**, places where merchants could bring their goods—hence our use of the word
"staple" to mean a basic commodity. Best of all, there is
the **ale-tastor**: "an officer sworn to look to . . . the good-
ness of bread and ale or beer." A tough job, but somebody
had to do it.

One also can't help but admire Cowell's use of certain
obsolete terms that are long overdue for a revival. The
Anglo-Saxon terms **backberond** (a thief caught carrying
pilfered goods on his back) and **miskenning** (misspeaking
in court) would both prove highly useful today. The dulcet
word **hoghenhine**, which denotes a houseguest who stays
more than two nights, after which the host must either
evict him or become legally responsible for him, would
come in handy around the holidays. And how impover-
ished is our language—if not our economy—without a
coin known as a **Gallihalpens**?

Cowell was a contemporary of Shakespeare, who was
himself so addicted to legal jargon that many scholars believe that the dramatist practiced, or at least studied, law in
his youth. Tucked away in the Bard's many plays and son-
nets are dozens of legal terms, including **pleading, plaintiff,
defendant, appellant,** and **jury,** to name just a few. Shakespeare's Sonnet 46, for example, depicts an imaginary lawsuit between the author's eye and his heart for possession
of a beloved woman. Here we get both **plead** and **plea,
defendant, title, quest** (short for inquest, or jury), **impan-
eled,** and **verdict**. The sonnet concludes with the jury

giving each party a **moiety** (a half interest): namely, the eye gets the beloved's outward beauty while the heart gets her inner love.

Legal English, like English itself, emerged from a melting pot of languages, including Anglo-Saxon, Norman French, and Church Latin. The word **law** is Norse in origin, a legacy of the Viking raids that led to permanent settlements in northern England. The word originally meant "that which is laid down," so don't bother laying down the law—it already is.

As one seventeenth-century observer noted, the laws of England "are as mixt as our language, compounded of British, Roman, Saxon, Danish [and] Norman customs. And as our language is so much the richer, so the laws are the more complete."

CROSSING THE POND

In the early United States, the link between law and language was as strong as it had been in England. The patriarch of all American dictionaries, Noah Webster (1758–1843), was a lawyer, although not particularly successful at that profession. His great contribution lay in the realization that America needed to declare its linguistic independence—especially when it came to legal language. In 1800 the leading British dictionary defined **escheat** (forfeiture of property to the state) as follows:

> Any lands, or other profits, that fall to a lord within his manor by forfeiture, or the death of his tenant, dying without heir general or especial.

Lord? Manor? That would hardly do for a republic. Webster stripped away the aristocratic verbiage to give us a democratic escheat: "The falling of lands to the owner or to the state by forfeiture or failure of heirs."

Webster cleaned up references to the Crown from other legal terms, approved such innovations as using **deed** as a verb, and introduced crucial American usages like **constitutionality**, a word first attributed to Alexander Hamilton. In all, Webster devoted more than twenty-five years to his dictionary, including two years of research in England. It remains a towering work of scholarship.

It would be nice to think of Webster as a kind, scholarly man in a fuzzy cardigan. Unfortunately, history remembers him as a "severe, correct, humorless, religious, temperate man who was not easy to like, even by other severe, religious, temperate, humorless people." It was not enough for Webster to produce a dictionary—the ex-lawyer wanted his definitions to have the backing of *law*. He pressed then–Chief Justice John Marshall to adopt his dictionary as the official dictionary of the Supreme Court. Marshall declined.

America soon had its own purpose-built law dictionaries, no thanks to Webster. The first, published in 1839, was the product of the French-born John Bouvier. Scores of competing dictionaries followed, including the most famous American law lexicon, *Black's Law Dictionary,* first published in 1891 and still in print today.

Nothing better illustrates American law's obsession with language than a series of books with the unassuming name *Words and Phrases.* Each page of *Words and Phrases* contains upward of twenty brief summaries of court decisions on the legal meaning of various, well, words and phrases. Each book in the series has about 800 pages, and there are 118 books. The entry for **shall**—not an especially ambiguous word, one might think—runs to 93 pages, citing more than twelve hundred cases.

TODAY'S LEGALESE

By the 1960s, the late Professor David Mellinkoff, a renowned authority on legal language, could state without exaggeration that "no profession of words has a longer history of practical effort devoted to refining language."

The results of all that refinement have been decidedly mixed. Remember the elegant law of King Ine? Well, thirteen hundred years later, British lawmakers have been reduced to writing statutes that say: "The hours of non-hours work worked by a worker in a pay reference period shall be the total of the number of hours spent by him during the pay reference period."

But that's nothing. When British regulators turned their attention to the subject of *nuts,* they produced a sentence of almost sublime absurdity:

> In the Nuts (unground)(other than Ground Nuts) Order the expression "nuts" shall have reference to such nuts, other than ground nuts, as would but for this amending Order not qualify as nuts (unground)(other than ground nuts) by reason of their being nuts (unground).

Meanwhile, in sunny Australia, a recent immigration law declares that "prescribed decisions of the Secretary [may be] reviewed by prescribed review officers on application, as prescribed, by prescribed persons." Perhaps the person who wrote *that* sentence needs a prescription.

The United States fares no better at writing laws. Taking a random page from the Code of Federal Regulations, one finds this bewildering pronouncement from the IRS:

> The fact that it may be difficult or impossible to provide a benefit, right, or feature described in paragraph (b)(3)(i) of this section under a plan of a different type than the plan or plans under which it is provided is one of the factors taken into account in determining whether the plan satisfies the effective availability requirement of §1.401(a)(4)-4(c)(1).

To which one can only say: Oh dear, is that the time?

We instinctively know legalese when we see it, but defining it is another matter. Certain traits of legal language seem obvious once you know them. For example, once you recognize that the law prefers nouns over verbs, you start to understand why a lawyer will always *bring a lawsuit* instead of *suing,* or *make an application* instead of *applying.* The process of turning verbs into nouns—linguists call it nominalization—is a useful tool for making things sound universal, for example, "cutting down trees is prohibited" rather than "you may not cut down trees." It also allows lawyers to fudge questions of personal responsibility: Why say "my client injured Mr. Smith on Tuesday" when you can say "Mr. Smith received an injury on Tuesday?"

The law's long-standing love affair with run-on sentences becomes less mysterious when one knows that law clerks were traditionally paid by the page. Originally the clerks simply inflated their documents by using ridiculously large margins and script. When judges got wise and started to impose rules about margin width, the clerks resorted to repetition and wordiness to puff up their fees. The legacy of the medieval scribes continues today: With lawyers paid by the hour, there is still little incentive to keep things short.

It doesn't take an expert to show that legal documents are difficult to read, but there are experts to confirm it just the same. One objective measure of readability is the Flesch Reading Ease Test, developed by Dr. Rudolph Flesch, author of *Why Johnny Can't Read*. The Flesch test is graded on a scale of 0 to 100, with 0 being very unclear and 100 being crystal clear. Somehow, the Social Security Act received a *negative* 130 on the Flesch Test, while the Ethics in Government Act weighed in at minus 219. Congress, you see, may have a willing spirit, but its Flesch is weak.

PLAIN VS. PRECISION:
A FIGHT TO THE DEATH

What is to be done with the language of the law? There are two opposing schools of thought on this question: "Precision" and "Plain English." And let's just say that if you belong to one of these groups, you don't want to wander onto the other side's turf after dark. Accidents do happen.

The Precision camp holds that the complexity of legal language flows naturally from the need of lawyers to be super precise. According to this theory, there is nothing to be done about legalese—it's fine just the way it is. The multiple subordinate clauses and technical jargon found in legal documents are there to describe highly complex relationships and to stamp out ambiguity.

The Precision School probably reached its zenith a few decades ago when, for example, one legal scholar exultantly praised legal textbooks as ranking "in the exactitude of their language with the classic studies in physics and natural science."

An even more arresting statement of the Precision school came from Sir Ernest Gowers, a British civil servant who proclaimed legal language to be "obscure in order that it may be unambiguous." In effect, the law beats me because it loves me. As recently as 1994, a law review article asked the question, "Should the main goal of statutory drafting be accuracy or clarity?" which assumes that making statutes clearer will make them less "accurate."

To all this talk of precision, Plain English flips an unceremonious bird. There is no structural reason, according to Plain English advocates, why the law cannot be written in simple, clear language.

Plain English embraces a number of different concepts, including using shorter sentences, active voice, and dropping surplus verbiage such as *hereafter, hereinbefore, thereto,* and words of that ilk. The underlying philosophy of the Plain English school is that ordinary citizens ought to be able to understand the laws they live under and the contracts they sign.

Plain English could just as easily be described as a crusade rather than a school of thought. This is particularly so in Britain, where one organization, the Plain English Campaign, has had a profound effect on the language of law and bureaucracy. Founded in the 1970s by a largely self-educated woman in Liverpool named Chrissie Maher, the campaign has had such notable successes as the banishment of Latin from England's civil courts.

A moment's thought will tell you that the Plain English school has the better of the argument with the Precision School. The sheer number of lawsuits arising from ambiguities in contracts and statutes is enough to suggest that legal language has not achieved its desired "precision" despite a millennium of effort. And the need for technical terms is almost certainly exaggerated. One law professor estimates that only 2 percent of the average legal document is actually devoted to conveying legal concepts. The other 98 percent needs our help.

But don't count out the Precision School just yet. In 1994, a Michigan lawyer denounced the "Plain English Jihad" for causing legal English to lose its "flavor and precision." More recently, the Scottish lawyer and academic Alfred Phillips bitterly attacked Plain English in his book *Lawyers' Language* (2003). For starters, Phillips goes to great pains to explain that "plain language" is a misnomer and should really be referred to as "ordinary language"— exactly the kind of niggling technicality that makes people hate lawyers.

Professor Phillips then tells us that he considers "ordinary language" to be just as dangerous as "plain language"—so why did he make such a fuss about the distinction in the first place? Heaven knows, but he offers the dire prediction that "were ordinary language generally to replace legal language in legal texts, any (dubious) gains in intelligibility would be wiped out by the loss of precision." He concludes that efforts to encourage plain English "are misguided and their failure is inevitable." After which, presumably, he unleashes his evil-professor laugh.

And now things start to get nasty, for there is a radical wing of the Plain English movement that regards people like Phillips as toadies of a vast legal-industrial conspiracy. The conspiracy theory dates back to the nineteenth-century philosopher Jeremy Bentham, who said that "the easiest way to create a monopoly is to invent a language and procedure which will be unintelligible to the layman. . . . In many ways it is . . . the art of the ancient and noble profession of the law."

The argument has been restated many times since Bentham. The contemporary British academic Peter Goodrich, for example, acidly argues that lawyers use "archaic" terminology in order to prop up "an economic elite and the discriminatory values that serve such an elite."

Intriguingly, there is some historical evidence to support the conspiracy theory. As we shall see in later chapters, English judges and lawyers continued to use French for many centuries after the Norman Conquest; almost certainly this had something to do with keeping tight control on the supply of legal services. In the sixteenth century, England's Attorney General, Sir Edward Coke, defended the use of French as a means of protecting the public, "lest the unlearned by bare reading . . . might suck out errors, and trusting in conceit, might endamage themselves." A similar argument was advanced by the legal reporter William Style, who in 1658 asserted that disseminating laws in English had led to "unquiet spirits" among the masses.

The idea of using legal language as a badge of exclusivity is not unique to English. Legend has it that the ancient Celtic lawyers of Britain and Ireland communicated in a language that was already archaic in Roman times. The ancient

Egyptians developed a special form of hieroglyphics—demotic script—specifically for law and government. Demotic has been called the "original legalese."

In Japan, there are two native writing systems, called *katakana* and *hiragana,* but historically most statutes are not written in either. Instead, Japanese laws were written in Chinese. It was only in this century that the Tokyo authorities even began translating some of the more important codes into Japanese. The situation in Greece is analogous. There, modern Greek (*Demotiki*) has all but displaced the ancient-style "pure" Greek (*Katharevousa*), which was for years the preferred language of scholarly discourse. As recently as 1995, Greek law was said to remain a "bastion" of the aristocratic *Katharevousa.*

Whether tidbits such as these add up to a conspiracy among lawyers is merely of historical interest. It is a little hard to believe that there is an active conspiracy among lawyers today. But the main debate—between the advocates of Precision and Plain English—is vitally important.

At stake is the future of "legal literacy," a measure of citizens' ability to read legal documents and understand the substance of legal proceedings. In 1996, Canadian researchers, using data from an international adult literacy survey, estimated that fewer than 25 percent of Canadians possessed legal literacy. Using the same methodology, the figure for the United States would be 18 to 21 percent.

The decline in legal literacy affects everyone's ability to know his or her rights, but it has its greatest impact on low-wage earners. In March 2005, the *New York Times* reported that fewer than 5 percent of the twenty million potential applicants were expected to apply for the government's new prescription drug benefit, because the forms were too complicated for people to understand. In Britain, thc Plain English Campaign estimates that *billions* of pounds of government benefits go unclaimed for the same reason.

The notion of informed consent—that is, a patient's approval of a medical procedure—has also been gutted by low legal literacy. One study estimates that only 3 to 20 percent of adults in the United States can actually give *informed* consent, largely because the required consent forms are chock-full of legalese. There are only two ways to boost legal literacy: Either make legal language more intelligible, or send everyone to law school.

Just how does legal language differ from everyday language, and how did it get that way? What are some of the plain English alternatives to the most common forms of legalese? And what, exactly, is a tort? These are some of the questions I aim to answer in this book. But first, you must read the fine print.

THE FINE PRINT

Bottomry: maritime law. A contract, in nature of a mortgage of a ship, on which the owner borrows money to enable him to fit out the ship . . .

— *BOUVIER'S LAW DICTIONARY* (6TH ED. 1856)

In 2005, Bayer Pharmaceuticals ran a series of television ads featuring a sultry brunette purring about the quality of her sex life ever since her boyfriend started taking Levitra. If you watched those commercials you may have been somewhat startled at the end when a voice-over sternly warns that "erections lasting longer than four hours require immediate medical attention."

Not to deny that an erection lasting longer than four hours requires immediate *something*—a medal perhaps?—but one wonders why a leading pharmaceutical company had to announce it on TV.

The answer, of course, is because lawyers told them to. The lawyers, in turn, are complying with the mandates of the U.S. Food and Drug Administration, which requires drug companies to disclose all possible side effects on product labeling as well as in advertising. In April 2005, the FDA had ordered Bayer to pull a shorter version of the commercial that lacked the necessary warning.

Product warnings are just one example of the **fine print** that lawyers have foisted on society. Such disclosures are designed as a very practical defense against future lawsuits—*You can't sue me for that four-hour erection, I warned you about that*—but as a matter of legal style, they border on the sublime. Who but a lawyer would insist that a fireplace log carry a label saying "Warning: Risk of Fire"? Or that sleeping pills "may cause drowsiness"? Or that one should "never iron clothes while they are being worn"?

As outrageous as the Levitra warnings may have seemed at first, they quickly fade, as all corporate disclosures do, into a kind of white noise. This is what happens to the fine

print: We take it for granted because it is endlessly repeated, such as the ubiquitous phrase "past performance
does not guarantee future results," meaning, presumably,
that just because you got one four-hour erection doesn't
mean you'll get another.

Legal language that gets copied from document to document is known as **boilerplate** and is, for some inexplica-
ble reason, always assumed to be harmless. Think about
the last time that a landlord or benefits administrator
asked you to sign a lengthy contract. He or she probably
told you not to worry about the actual words because "it's
only boilerplate." That sort of advice is, I need hardly tell
you, sheer poppycock. Contracts are meant to do things. If
the boilerplate provision actually does something, then
you ought to understand it; if it doesn't do anything, then
you should cross it out, which is guaranteed to bring
howls of protest from the laid-back "it's only boilerplate"
guy on the other side of the table.

ABSOLUTELY RIVETING!

The term "boilerplate" originated in the offices of
nineteenth-century American newspapers. Back then, newspapers were printed from metal plates that were cast from
mats (short for matrices) made by the paper's typesetters.
Some of the savvier news agencies and syndicates would
send out their press releases or columns in precast metal
plates that could not be altered. Editors referred to these
prepackaged plates as "boilerplate" because they resembled
the standard-sized iron plates that were riveted together to
make boilers. Over time, boilerplate came to mean any part
of a newspaper that remained unchanged, issue after issue.

At least, that's the most often cited derivation of the word. A competing theory has it that the term was originally coined in honor of the American Press Association, one of the earliest press syndicates, which in 1892 began its life in a building that also housed a sheet-iron factory. Chicago printers dubbed the APA's offices "the boilerplate factory."

Whatever its exact etymology, boilerplate became a journalistic cliché. At some point in the last century, lawyers borrowed the term from the field of journalism, and they have yet to give it back.

Boilerplate is all around us, particularly in the kinds of documents that ordinary people deal with on a daily basis; think leases, mortgages, promissory notes, insurance policies, membership agreements, subpoenas, powers of attorney, and so on. It is through boilerplate that most ordinary people come to know—and hate—legalese.

What distinguishes boilerplate is its combination of archaic terminology and frenzied verbosity, as though it were written by a medieval scribe on crack. A prime example of boilerplate is the archly old-fashioned tendency to refer to the signers of a contract as **the party of the first part** and **the party of the second part**. Although those terms are of nineteenth-century vintage, one study confirmed that lawyers continued to use them at least into the 1980s—no doubt because they were simply copying and pasting familiar boilerplate.

In the 1935 movie *A Night at the Opera,* the Marx Brothers rip such language to shreds—literally. Groucho, who is trying to lure Chico into signing a contract, reads the first clause aloud: "The party of the first part shall be known in this contract as the party of the first part." Chico doesn't like the sound of that, and so they agree to rip that part of the contract out. And on they go tearing out clauses up through "the party of the ninth part."

After tearing up most of the contract, Groucho and Chico disagree about the final clause: "If any of the parties participating in this contract is shown not to be in their right mind, the entire agreement is automatically nullified." Groucho offers the classic defense of boilerplate: "It's all right, that's in every contract. That's what they call a 'sanity clause.' " To which Chico defiantly answers: "You can't fool me! There ain't no Sanity Clause!"

The Precision School has risen to the defense of the party of the first part. In his 2002 article, "Against Plain English," University of Houston law professor David Crump describes such terms as being "useful" in consumer contracts. What he means is that these abstract terms make it easier for lawyers to churn out contracts—because they don't have to go to the trouble of inserting real names into the documents—even though the lack of real names "prevents easy understanding" by the consumer. With all the consumer watchdogs in the world, it's refreshing to know that there is at least one lawyer watchdog.

MINDLESS REPETITION, ANYONE?

Truth be told, "the party of the first part" is hardly the most antiquated bit of boilerplate floating around these days. Insurance contracts, for example, routinely use the word **witnesseth**, which is merely an Old English form of the verb "to witness," as in "this policy witnesseth that. . . ." Many leases also use that word, as seen in the opening line, "Witnesseth: the lessor agrees to lease said property," etc., etc. Loyola law professor and plain-language advocate Peter Tiersma describes witnesseth as "a totemic signal that roughly means 'This is a legal contract; the following are its terms.'"

Not to deny that there is something fun and whimsical about throwing around Old English phrases. Just saying "witnesseth" is enough to summon up images of feudal lords, jousting, and great steins of beer delivered by lusty serving wenches. But on the whole, such fantasies are best indulged at your local Renaissance Faire. Witnesseth serves absolutely no purpose in today's contracts. Even if you update it to "witnesses" or "witness," it still adds nothing to the lease or insurance policy.

Similarly useless is the statement found at the end of many boilerplate **affidavits** (sworn statements): **Further affiant sayeth naught**—"naught" being an archaic term for "nothing." Since these words are always at the end of an affidavit, it is not as though they clarify some ambiguity. Anybody who gets to the end of the document will know exactly when you have nothing more to sayeth.

About half the time, lawyers mistakenly use the word "not" instead of "naught." Literally, the phrase "further affiant sayeth not" means "the affiant has one more thing to say: not," which would leave the affidavit with a strange hint of negation. The fact that no court in the land cares whether you write "naught" or "not" demonstrates that the phrase is pure surplusage and should just be left out entirely.

Why do some contracts have the word **indenture** at the top? It is because in ancient times certain contracts would be executed in two copies, each with matching notches or indentations at the top of the page. At a later time, the edges of the two pages could be brought together to show that they were part of the same agreement. "Indenture" and "indentation" both come from the Latin *dentatus* (having teeth), an etymology that nicely evokes the image of the serrated documents. These days, however, the word serves no purpose as an indenture is never actually indented, even when there are multiple copies. Now we have photocopiers.

The printing press exacerbated the law's natural tendency to preserve old phrases. Almost as soon as Gutenberg's first Bible rolled off the press (1455), English lawyers were putting together **formbooks**, that is, collections of sample contracts, pleadings, and other documents that had already passed muster with some court or another. Provided that one copied the form verbatim, no sporting judge could object. Formbooks continue to thrive to this day—even though the "books" may be CDs or downloadable files—in a language reminiscent of Henry VIII.

The only lasting benefit of the formbooks—and the boilerplate they contain—is that they afford an almost archaeological cross section of the history of legal language. From the Old English period (pre-1100), as we've seen, there are such delicious leftovers as witnesseth and sayeth.

Much more prevalent are the vestiges of the Middle English period (roughly 1100–1500). This was the language's formative age, when Oxford and Cambridge were founded and Chaucer wrote *The Canterbury Tales*. The spirit of the day was one of experimentation. Lawyers and other literate folk enjoyed nothing better—or so it seems to us today—than inventing new words by putting together two or more old ones, such as the very legal-sounding **notwithstanding**. To this generation we owe the profusion of **where**- words in legal documents: *whereas, wherefore,* and *whereunder,* for example, which can still be found in legal boilerplate, as well as some interesting forms that did not survive: *wherehence, whereafterward,* and *wheretil.* Of similar vintage are the **here**- words: *herein, hereunder,* and so on.

The spellings of these words have been updated to conform to modern conventions. In the Middle Ages, spelling was a free-for-all; one writer could spell the same word several different ways in the course of a single document. A word like "where" had wildly inconsistent spellings in medieval England, including *hwaer, huer, quare, gwhare, hwore,* and even *whore.*

The odd invocation to be found at the beginning of many legal documents, including bonds and powers of attorney, **Know all men by these presents**, also comes from this period. The phrase **these presents** does not refer to gifts, but is a translation of the Latin *presens scriptum* ("this writing"). As with witnesseth, the function of "these presents" is purely ritualistic: "Look out—here comes a legal document!"

Not all Latin was translated into English. Even more than today, medieval lawyers used Latin for all kinds of documents. The scribes developed a system of abbreviating legal Latin known as "court hand." The system was ingenious; rather too ingenious, in fact, since the meaning behind some of the abbreviations was forgotten entirely. This is true of the abbreviation **ss**. These two little letters appear at the beginning of virtually every affidavit filed in the United States despite the fact that nobody knows for certain what they stand for. Seriously: "ss" is sometimes said to be short for *scilicet* ("one may know"); other suggestions include *subscripsi, sans, sacerdotes, sanctissimus, Spiritus Sanctus,* and *sunt. Black's Law Dictionary* will only go so far as to say that it is "supposed to be a contraction of *'scilicet.'* " And yet, no self-respecting lawyer will draft an affidavit without it.

Members of the Precision School cling to Old and Middle English expressions as though they were life preservers in a sea of ambiguity. In one journal, a retired lawyer defended the phrase "I *hereby* certify," rather than plain old "I certify" because the *hereby* clarifies "I, right now, by this document, certify, etc." He then conceded that when a document says "I certify," there can hardly be any ambiguity as to the "right now, by this document" part. Still, said the lawyer, "it never hurts to emphasize this fact." And, he added, words such as *hereby* and *herein* are valuable—even if they are not precise—because they "demand the respect of the reader."

None of this holds water. The whole kit and caboodle of Olde English expressions smacks of needless pedantry. One suspects that people who use words like "heretofore" are the sort of people who say "I intend to perambulate to an adjacent hostelry for a frosty libation" instead of "I'm going to the corner for a beer."

OOH LAW LAW

French terms flooded into the law during the Middle English period, and remain fixed in our legal formulas today. After 1066, Norman French had become the language of the court and nobility. Lawyers, who knew all about the power of words, adopted the aristocracy's language. It took a generation or two, but the legal profession gradually merged with the upper classes into a francophone elite.

The proliferation of French also made it fashionable to put the noun before the adjective (it's *le style français*) and a number of legal phrases retain the inverted word order, such as **attorney general, court martial, accounts payable,** and **fee simple**.

The age of "law French" was also the beginning of the diabolical Precision School of legal language, for many lawyers justified the use of French on the grounds that it was inherently more precise than English for expressing legal concepts. As late as 1824, an English barrister could proclaim that "the law is scarce expressible properly in English." The historian Sir William Holdsworth wistfully described the Middle English period as one in which "the common lawyer had in his law French a technical language equal in precision to that of the [continental lawyers]."

Toward the end of this era, as fewer and fewer Englishmen spoke French fluently, lawyers fumbled about in an increasingly comical patois—court records of the seventeenth century reveal such franglais expressions as "beat le dogg" and "fetch un sword." As you will have guessed, legal language was becoming a bilingual affair.

The passion for bilingualism left English law with a tradition of double-barreled phrases—**breaking and entering, fit and proper, free and clear**—each created by combining English and French synonyms. Consider the following list (French-derived words in italics):

breaking and *entering*
fit and *proper*
free and *clear*
goods and *chattels*

had and *received*
peace and quiet
right, title, and *interest*
will and *testament*

Less well known than Latin or French, Hebrew also left its mark on legal English. The traditional formula in loan documents—that the borrower pledges "all my goods, moveable and immoveable" is a translation of the Jewish *shetar* (covenant). In medieval England, only Jews were allowed to lend money at interest, and these transactions were memorialized in the *shetar*s, or, as the English called them, **starra**. The starra were kept in a special chamber in the English Exchequer—this room was the **Star Chamber** that was later made famous when it became the meeting place of a secret court that tried high crimes (more on those in Chapter 6).

FORMS FOLLOW FUNCTION

Now that formbooks were coming hot off the printing press (post-1500), every lawyer had ready access to a common set of **precedents**, or *presidents,* as the word was sometimes spelled. A precedent literally means "that which came before," and it is pretty much the key to the way lawyers think. Courts in the English-speaking world follow the precedents laid down by earlier decisions. And lawyers, when drafting documents, always prefer to use a precedent rather than writing something from scratch. This is not merely a matter of convenience, but one of caution. Any form that has found its way into a book must be one that "works."

The formbooks were smash hits with the legal profession. As a result, all of the linguistic oddities discussed above, and many more, became set in stone, carefully preserved, and passed on from one generation to the next. When the British colonized North America, English law and English formbooks came with the package.

Until the late eighteenth century, American lawyers borrowed from British formbooks, but after independence, they began to clamor for something a little more home-grown. In 1797, New Jersey lawyer William Griffith promised to give them just that with his *Scrivener's Guide*— the title alone gives one goose bumps. It turns out the book was only a slightly changed version of an English book of the same name, advertised as being "Useful for all Gentlemen, especially those that Practice the Law."

The same was true of Joseph Story's *A Selection of Pleadings in Civil Actions* (1805), which promised to give "American" precedents but consisted mainly of recycled English forms. The fact was that American practice was so closely modeled on the British that uniquely American forms, although appealing to the patriotic spirit, scarcely existed.

Later in the nineteenth century, legal publishers realized that they could vastly increase sales by pitching their books to the general public. Thus *Everybody's Lawyer and Book of Forms,* written by a Philadelphia lawyer in 1869, promised that every man could be his own lawyer— provided he bought the book. *Everybody's Lawyer* also made the bold claim, "In no instance has injury or loss resulted to anyone from [this book's] use." Which may well have been true, but it is also unlikely that the book caused anyone to get a four-hour erection.

"Superstition" would be the best word to describe the law's attitude toward forms. Like a gambler unwilling to wash his lucky shirt lest it lose some of its magic, the average lawyer wouldn't change a comma in a trusted boilerplate form. In Australia, a corporate executive once tried to rewrite one of her company's standard form contracts. Where the existing contract said:

> The Agreement shall **commence** on _____
> and **expire** on _____,

the executive wanted to replace commence and expire with **start** and **finish**. The company's legal department objected to the proposal, contending that *start* and *finish* "do not yet have established meanings" in law.

In a 1999 law journal article, a Michigan lawyer named David Daly proposed improvements to a standard **indemnification clause**, by which one person promises to compensate another person for loss. The standard provision stated that "the indemnifying party [may select] counsel satisfactory to [the] **indemnified party**." Daly proposed to replace that with a sentence saying that the indemnifying party "may select counsel satisfactory to the **other party**." Although there could be no doubt as to the identity of the "other party" in the context, another lawyer wrote to the editor of the journal protesting that Daly's revisions had upset the "legal relations" described in the document.

Academic law journals feature scientific-sounding studies of boilerplate forms—and with titles like "Standardization and Innovation in Corporate Contracting" to choose from, why should anyone suffer from insomnia?

The results of these studies are often blindingly obvious. One journal declares, "Deletions generally must meet a high threshold of justification. . . . But inclusion of new boilerplate . . . requires much less justification." In other words, lawyers tend to add new language to existing forms without deleting any of the old language. The ones who add the most boilerplate end up with a reputation for being "precise."

What's more, lawyers often preface a new bit of boilerplate with the phrase "anything else in this agreement to the contrary notwithstanding" or words to that effect, meaning, "*this* clause trumps any other clause in the contract that is inconsistent with it." If you use that phrase more than once in the same form, things get very complicated.

If they can send a man to the moon, why can't they fix boilerplate? The Precision School argues that cutting out boilerplate will lead to fatal ambiguity. Others claim, ingeniously, that *clients* are to blame because they expect their lawyers to produce documents bristling with legalese. If they don't, the clients think they haven't got their money's worth. Although this may be true in some cases, the majority of clients would probably be happy with plain language. The problem is, they don't want to pay for it. Writing a plain English contract from scratch takes far more billable hours than cutting and pasting boilerplate. Few lawyers have the gumption to ask their clients to pay extra for plain English contracts when the boilerplate versions will get the job done.

It may be that lawyers earnestly plan to clean up the forms, remove the excess verbiage, and make their documents more user-friendly just as soon as they have some free time. Although that doesn't sound like a very appealing weekend project, one Chicago law professor reports that "many lawyers" "fantasize about the perfect form." They ought to get out more.

DELIVER US FROM
GOBBLEDYGOOK

Is there anyone who can reform all the tedious fine print clogging our lives? Are we doomed to suffer from unreadable contracts? Must we abandon all hope?

Wait—what's that sound in the distance? Could it be the Plain English cavalry?

Plain English advocates have made it a priority to improve consumer contracts for the compelling reason that these are the contracts that have the widest impact *and* the most egregious legalese.

Professor Tiersma cites an example from a lease: *the rent hereinbefore reserved and agreed to be paid.* As Tiersma elegantly explains, you could replace that whole mess of words with *the rent* without any loss of meaning. Precision advocates will bemoan the loss of "hereinbefore," but such words rarely add clarity to a sentence. Consider the English case of *Bengough* v. *Edridge* (1827), in which the phrase "hereinafter" in a will was treated as meaning "hereinbefore."

In the United States, plain language reform began in earnest in the 1970s, when Citibank decided, on its own initiative, to try out a plain language version of a **promissory note** (a piece of paper that you have to sign when you borrow money). The change was breathtaking. The new promissory note said things like:

You can delay enforcing any of your rights under this note without losing them.

Which may not seem all that impressive, until you consider that it replaced the following babble from the old promissory note:

> No failure or delay on the part of the Bank in exercising, and no failure to file or otherwise enforce the Bank's security interest in or with respect to any Collateral, shall operate as a waiver of any right or remedy hereunder or release any of the undersigned, and the Obligations of the undersigned may be extended or waived by the Bank, any contract or other agreement evidencing or relating to any Obligation or any Collateral may be amended and any Collateral exchanged, surrendered or otherwise dealt with in accordance with any agreement relative thereto, all without affecting the liability of any of the undersigned.

The public appreciated the effort, and politicians took notice. In 1978, New York State enacted America's first general plain language law. Today, most states have laws requiring plain English in consumer documents. Incidentally, the lawyer who got the ball rolling at Citibank was a young man named Duncan MacDonald, who, only five years before he rewrote the promissory note, had received a C from a law school writing instructor who objected to his unconventional ideas.

In Britain, the Office of Fair Trading, no doubt spurred on by the Plain English Campaign, has published rules for writing clear consumer contracts, as well as before-and-after examples of typical boilerplate provisions translated into plain English. Some examples:

> **Old provision:** This Agreement and the benefits and advantages herein contained are personal to the Member and shall not be sold, assigned or transferred by the Member.
>
> **Translation:** Membership is not transferable.
>
> **Old provision:** Title to property in the goods shall remain vested in the Company (notwithstanding the delivery of the same to the Consumer) until the price of the Goods comprised in the contract and all other money due from the Customer to the Company on any other account has been paid in full.
>
> **Translation:** We shall retain ownership of the goods until you have finished paying for them.

With all these spirited initiatives, one might well ask why the world is still full of unreadable contracts. The problem is that plain language is an easy concept to describe, but a difficult one to legislate. New York takes a general approach, requiring that "the writing be clear and coherent and the words used have common and everyday meaning." Which is all well and good, but obviously has a **loophole** through which you can **drive a truck** (if you're an American lawyer) or a **coach and horses** (if you're British), since "clear and coherent" exists in the eyes of the beholder.

Other states have enacted detailed requirements for plain language, such as minimizing passive sentences, prohibiting certain technical terms, and specifying the maximum length of sentences and paragraphs. Connecticut even mandates the average number of syllables per word (1.55). Still other states rely on readability tests, such as the Flesch Reading Ease Test that we discussed in Chapter 1. Ohio, for example, requires that insurance policies receive a minimum score of 40 on the Flesch test; in Florida the minimum is 45.

As much as one applauds these laws, we still have a long way to go. I found two contracts in my files at home that claim to be written in "Plain English Format." One is a lease that uses such plain English expressions as "material misstatement of fact" (a phrase you will no doubt remember from the film *Sex, Material Misstatements of Fact, and Videotape*). The lease also suffers from legalistic redundancy, such as the insistence that rent be paid "in full *without deduction*" or that the landlord shall not be liable for "loss, expense, or damage." There is slightly sinister ambiguity, such as when the landlord is given the right to "enter the apartment at reasonable hours to: repair, inspect, [or] *exterminate*." Pests, one hopes.

The other "plain English" document in my files is an insurance policy. The list of losses that are excluded from coverage includes "Gradual *or* sudden loss," which, when you think about it, pretty much covers the field. Despite the promise of plain language, the policy gets increasingly bollixed up with legalese as each paragraph drags on and on. By page six, we find a provision—likely a piece of inherited boilerplate—that includes *aforesaid, therein, within described, premises, thereon,* and the splendidly redundant *null and void*.

Plain English has a certain indefinable something that no set of rules can ever capture. The effort to do so is reminiscent of many companies' attempts to define "business casual" dress. In the late 1990s, one New York law firm issued a three-page memo describing in exquisite detail the characteristics of acceptable business casual dress. A senior partner showed up at a firm event wearing his pajamas, explaining—quite correctly—that they conformed perfectly to the business casual criteria.

Plain English is a little bit like business casual; it's a matter of style. And even when you achieve a fitting style, there is no guarantee that your plain English document won't end up embroiled in a lawsuit, which, conveniently enough, is the subject of the next chapter.

3

LADIES AND GENTLEMEN OF THE JURY

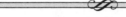

Vexatious litigation: n. baseless litigation commenced only to annoy and harass the defendant.

— RANDOM HOUSE WEBSTER'S DICTIONARY
OF THE LAW (2000)

Richard Mylward was an aspiring lawyer in Elizabethan England. In the spring of 1596, his father decided to sue somebody named Weldon and, naturally enough, hired Richard to represent him.

Eager to impress his father, or the judge, or both, Richard produced a **brief** totaling an extraordinary 120 pages. On a fine May morning—perhaps a bird was singing?—Richard marched to the courthouse in Westminster Hall and presented his brief.

The judge was not impressed. In fact, he reckoned that all the relevant information would have fit in sixteen pages, leaving 104 pages of useless drivel. As a punishment, he ordered that a court official cut a hole in the middle of the brief and put Richard's head through it. Richard was then to be paraded around Westminster Hall "bareheaded and barefaced" and with his head poking out from his brief in cartoon fashion.

Wouldn't it be nice if more judges followed the example of *Mylward* v. *Weldon*? Some wish they could. Almost exactly four hundred years after that great decision, a federal judge in New York lamented that wading through a seventy-page brief "stirs nostalgia" for the "rigors" of the Mylward case.

VITA BREVIS, DOCUMENT LONGER

A **brief** is a written argument that is submitted to a court as part of a lawsuit, and it is a fair question to ask why something called a brief is usually anything but. Granted, "brief" is related to the Latin *brevis,* meaning short. Its immediate ancestor, however, is the noun *breve,* which refers to a letter issued by the Pope, less solemn than a papal bull, but authoritative nonetheless. This is where we get the legal sense of brief, which was originally synonymous with **writ**, an old-fashioned term for a document that initiates a lawsuit.

So a brief is not by definition a short document, but it doesn't have to be a long one either. In America, up to the early twentieth century, legal briefs typically consisted of just a few pages of legal citations and argument. In the 1908 case of *Muller* v. *Oregon,* a prominent Boston lawyer named Louis Brandeis caused a sensation by submitting a 113-page brief, bristling not only with case citations, but with medical and legal statistics to support his argument. After Brandeis won the Muller case, courtrooms across the country were flooded with briefs resembling Homeric epics; they became known as **Brandeis briefs**. And what was Brandeis's punishment for dragging the profession back to the dark days of *Mylward?* Disgrace? Ruin? Disbarment? He was elevated to the United States Supreme Court.

Not all courts welcomed Brandeis briefs. In 1917, then–Supreme Court justice Oliver Wendell Holmes complained to a British colleague, "I abhor, loathe and despise these long discourses"—itself a fine example of three adjectives doing the job of one. In 1992, a federal court imposed fines, known as **sanctions**, against a lawyer who submitted "voluminous briefs" and "long tedious affidavits." In an attempt to defend his conduct, the lawyer submitted yet another brief—this one 158 pages long.

Briefs and lawsuits are part of the fabric of American life, for ours is a **litigious** society. **Litigation**, by the way, is just a five-dollar word describing any dispute that might end up in court. The word comes from the Latin *litigare,* which means "to quarrel." The word has been used in the sense of "carrying on a lawsuit" since the seventeenth century and has spawned the words **litigant**, a party to a lawsuit, and **litigator**, a lawyer who specializes in this field.

Lawsuit itself is a curious term. It comes from the Latin *secta,* which means followers. In the Middle Ages, a litigant was required to bring a group of followers to court to vouch for the truth of his statements. This requirement was eventually dropped; however, in classic fashion, the language remained frozen. Law clerks continued to refer to the act of starting a court case as bringing a *secta,* which, over time, was translated into the English (via Old French) *suite.* By the seventeenth century, the term had morphed into law-suite and then law-suit, and finally the unhyphenated word we have today.

Most lawsuits are **civil** suits. Not civil in the sense of civility, but in the sense of civil war—they take place between fellow citizens. Litigation that pits the State against one or more citizens is **criminal** (more on that in Chapter 6).

PLAINT THE TOWN RED

Lawsuits start with a **complaint**. I don't mean peevish whining, although there's usually plenty of that. A complaint is a formal document that sets a lawsuit in motion. The person who files a complaint is called a **plaintiff**, except in criminal cases, where it is the **prosecutor** (from Latin *prosequi,* to pursue). Viewing "complaint" and "plaintiff" together, one can see they have a common root: *plaint,* an archaic word meaning "lamentation," ultimately from the Latin verb *plangere,* meaning "to beat one's breast." In modern English, the adjective form of plaint—plaintive—still denotes a general sense of sorrow, while the noun plaintiff is strictly a law term.

The person being sued is the **defendant**. The defendant has to answer the complaint with a document called, with admirable clarity, an **answer**. Complaints and answers are known as **pleadings**. Because pleadings are the first documents submitted in a litigation, judges have always scrutinized them very closely, looking for any excuse to dismiss the case on a technicality. Over the years, the rules of pleading became very demanding; as we'll see in Chapter 6, criminal cases have been tossed out over fine points of grammar and spelling—Latin spelling at that.

In two nineteenth-century British cases, success or failure came down to the difference between vowels and consonants. In *Kinnersly* v. *Knott,* the pleading was dismissed because it identified the defendant as "John M. Knott," and "M," said the court, is not a name. By contrast, in *Lomax* v. *Landells,* the pleading passed muster even though it referred to a person as "I. Williams." The judge explained: "A name must consist of a word. Every vowel is a word and may be pronounced separately; a consonant cannot be pronounced without the aid of a vowel." Thus "I" is a name even though "M" is not.

This neat distinction did not last long. Just two years after the Lomax case, another English judge reopened the vowel vs. consonant debate, observing, "There is no doubt that a vowel can be a good Christian name; why not a consonant? I have been informed by a gentleman of the bar . . . that he knows a lady who was baptized by the name of 'D.'"

One way to get past the hypertechnical courts is to load your pleading with boilerplate (see Chapter 2). As with all boilerplate, the logic for pleadings is that any language that has been accepted by one court can safely be submitted to another court. But this strategy can backfire if you carelessly cut and paste boilerplate from one complaint to another. In 2001, a lawyer filed a complaint accusing Microsoft of preventing other computer makers "from obtaining the supply of . . . generic drugs' active pharmaceutical treatment," which seems unlikely. Then again, who knows? Maybe Bill Gates actually has cornered the market on generic pharmaceuticals.

TRIAL AND ERROR

A **trial** is the culmination of litigation, in which a court applies the law to the facts and reaches a decision. A lawyer who regularly brings cases to trial is called a **trial lawyer**; in other words, a lawyer who **tries cases**. And tries and tries again.

Strange as it may seem, many perfectly good litigators are not trial lawyers, and they don't need to be. The reason for this is that very, very few litigations make it to trial. Most are **settled** outside of court.

But outside of which court? The United States has a dizzying variety. In the federal system, trials are held in **district court**, with appeals going to the **court of appeals**, and ultimately to the **Supreme Court**. The federal government also maintains a vast system of specialized courts, including the **bankruptcy court**, **tax court**, **immigration court**, the **Court of International Trade**, and dozens of other tribunals. Ever since 1934, the federal government has encouraged Indian tribes to create their own judicial systems; about 275 tribes have done so, creating courts with such colorful names as the **Healing to Wellness Court**.

As far as state courts go, there is absolutely no uniformity in what they call themselves. Some states follow the federal system, with district courts being the lowest level and supreme court being the highest, but you're just as likely to encounter **civil courts, circuit courts, county courts, courts of general session**, and (in Colorado) **Water Courts**. One of the most popular names is **superior court**, which, despite the sound of it, is actually a low-level court. In what seems like a deliberate attempt to confound nonlawyers, the State of New York refers to its lowest-level court as the **Supreme Court**—although that fact has become better known in recent years thanks to TV's *Law and Order*.

In Delaware, Pennsylvania, and Ohio, the trial court is known as the **Court of Common Pleas**, an ancient English name that derives from the Magna Carta (clause 17, to be exact), which called for the creation of a court to hear lawsuits in which the king had no direct interest. Historically, the chief clerk of the Common Pleas court was known as the **prothonotary**, a title that still survives in Pennsylvania. In England, however, the Court of Common Pleas and the office of prothonotary were abolished in the nineteenth century.

Delaware has a **Chancery Court**, so called because it is the descendant of the English courts that enforced the laws of the Chancellor of the Exchequer—a distinct set of rules known as **equity**. The Delaware Chancery Court is famous for the quality of its judges, particularly in commercial matters. Of course, not just anybody can take advantage of this court—you have to come within the court's jurisdiction, or its sphere of power. How do you know whether you qualify for the Chancery Court? According to the court's own website, the test is whether your case is the kind of case that would have been heard by the British High Court of Chancery before 1776—not necessarily a simple matter when dealing with leveraged buyouts, proxy contests, and other transactions that did not exist in the eighteenth century. Interestingly enough, the United Kingdom has not had a separate court of chancery since 1875.

This is not to say that the English have always been good at weeding out archaic legal usages—after all, British barristers still wear horsehair wigs in court. The medieval **Court of Chivalry** proved to be especially resilient, convening for the last time in 1955 to decide a dispute over a theater's right to use the City of Manchester's coat of arms. Even better was the **Piepowder Court**, with jurisdiction over disputes arising from traveling fairs and markets. The name refers to the dusty feet (*pieds poudrés* in French) of the itinerant merchants who appeared before that court. The last Piepowder Court survived in Bristol until abolished by legislation in 1971, much to the impoverishment of legal English.

WERE YOU LYING THEN, OR ARE YOU LYING NOW?

If you live in the United States, chances are you've been involved in litigation one way or another. In fact, millions of Americans are plaintiffs without even knowing it, through the device of **class actions**.

In a class action, a group of enterprising lawyers persuade a judge to certify a "class" of plaintiffs—for example, all men who suffered from four-hour erections in the past year—and then proceed to bring a lawsuit on behalf of the class. If you're a member of the class, you'll get a letter giving you the right to "opt out" of the class. Most likely, you'll throw the letter away without reading it because—you guessed it—it's written in legalese. Since you didn't opt out, you're a plaintiff. And if the defendant ends up paying money, you'll get your share, but it's usually a very small one.

In April 2005, a *Los Angeles Times* reporter was surprised to discover that his son had been a plaintiff in a class action lawsuit against Bank of America. The son was equally surprised, and disappointed, to learn that his cut would be 49 cents, while the plaintiffs' lawyers collected fees in excess of $2 million. In a similar action against Citibank, unwitting plaintiffs reported receiving checks as small as 2 cents. The legal fees were over $7 million.

Perhaps the best that can be said about being a class action plaintiff is that it does not require setting foot inside a courtroom. Indeed, for most nonlawyers and even for many lawyers, the only opportunity to see a full-fledged trial comes via serving on a **jury**.

Trial by jury was a medieval invention and, some would say, remains a distinctly medieval spectacle. For centuries, the British determined guilt and innocence by the **ordeal**, such as the ordeal by water—if she floats, she's a witch—and the ordeal by fire (cousin to today's commonly-invoked "trial by fire"), in which the accused had to walk nine paces with a red-hot iron in both hands.

Another method of dispute resolution, **trial by battle**, or **battel**, was imported to England by the Norman conquerors. Although not distinguished by verbal jousting, trial by battle had its own technical rules of pleading. A man accused of a crime could demand a battle by pleading "not guilty" followed by the words "and I will defend the same by my body." After which he would have to throw down his **gauntlet** (an armored glove).

In 1215, the Catholic Church effectively abolished trial by ordeal. Suddenly, authorities all over Europe had to find an equally scientific way to determine innocence and guilt—a tall order at a time when bloodletting represented the latest in medical technology. British jurists hit upon the novel idea of rounding up twelve local men and making them swear to tell the truth. The twelve men were called a jury, from the Old French word *jurée,* and ultimately, from the Latin *jurare,* meaning "to swear." *Jurare,* by the way, is also the root of **jurat**, a word that is still inserted at the end of many boilerplate affidavits, next to the notary public's signature.

You might have noticed that the Church did not abolish trial by battle, but only trial by ordeal. The right to a battle was hardly ever invoked after the fifteenth century, but it remained a legal option in England until 1819. In that year, a man named Abraham Thornton stood accused of murdering young Mary Ashford, whose elder brother William pressed charges. On November 17, 1817, Thornton appeared in the Court of King's Bench and was asked to enter a plea. He entered a plea of not guilty and challenged Ashford's brother to a battle. He then threw down a large gauntlet, presumably to the astonishment of all present. The case against Thornton was dismissed and Parliament rushed through legislation to ban trial by battle.

There is a postscript. The Act of 1819 applied only to

England and Wales. In 1985 two brothers on trial in Scotland invoked their right to trial by battle against the Queen's champion. The court, however, decided that the right to trial by battle no longer existed in Scotland, and even if it did, the brothers had failed to throw down a gauntlet. So there.

Originally jurors acted essentially as witnesses and were required to testify to facts, or at least to repeat neighborhood gossip. It wasn't until the sixteenth century that the English perfected a separate system for compelling the testimony of witnesses at trial using the **subpoena** (Latin for "under penalty"), which allowed for a clear separation between the jury and the witnesses. Finally, jurors could sit back and listen to other people talk. And talk, and talk.

The good news for jurors is that trial lawyers are, by a long measure, the most entertaining variety of lawyer, although a few hours of watching Court TV will be enough to show you that they rarely achieve cinematic levels of excitement. This is unfortunate, particularly since I decided to become a lawyer when I was in college after watching Charles Laughton conduct a brilliant cross-examination in the classic film *Witness for the Prosecution*. It was some years before I learned that real-life law practice offers few opportunities to reduce a witness to tears with a leering "Were you lying then, or are you lying now?"

Still, trials do offer moments of genuine poetry. One reason for this is that trial lawyers are specifically trained to use rhetorical devices such as rhyming and alliteration to drive their message home. The most famous example of this sort of language came from the late Johnnie Cochran, who, during the O.J. Simpson trial, used rhyme ("If it doesn't fit, you must acquit") and alliteration (the prosecution's evidence was "compromised, contaminated, and corrupted") to great effect.

Cochran was participating in one of the law's most venerated traditions. Both the ancient Celts and the Anglo-Saxons expressed their laws in semipoetic verses, using the same bag of linguistic tricks as Cochran did. The Anglo-Saxons, for example, had the following rhyming maxim:

Wo so boleth myn kyn
Ewerc is the calf myn

or, "whoever bulls my cow, the calf is mine," a phrase that speaks volumes about how Englishmen passed the time in the Middle Ages. The tradition of alliteration lives on in many common legal phrases: **aid and abet**; **clear and convincing**; **rest, residue, and remainder**. And poetic rhythm can still be heard in the witness's oath to tell **the truth, the whole truth, and nothing but the truth**.

TWELVE ANGRY (AND CONFUSED) MEN

After the lawyers have finished their entertainment, but before the jury can start deliberating, the judge recites the **jury instructions**. This means that the judge explains to the jury the various legal rules that they must apply to the facts of the case. That the instructions tend to be bone-dry and tedious documents is an added benefit of jury service.

Quite often, judges have no choice in the matter, because they are required to rely on **standard** or **pattern** jury instructions, written by long-forgotten committees of men in starched collars and frock coats. They are scrupulous in describing the law, and about as clear as the instructions for filling out your tax return. One federal judge, speaking seventy years ago, described jury instructions as "a foreign language"—a comment not entirely fair to foreigners.

Studies and anecdotal evidence confirm that jurors routinely get confused by legalese, interpreting **proximate cause** (the direct cause of an event) as "approximate cause" and **preponderance of the evidence** (proof that something is more likely than not) as "pondering the evidence." One jury decided that murder committed with **malice aforethought** meant murder committed with a mallet (see Chapter 6 for the real meaning). Oh well, six of one, twenty-to-life of the other.

The price of confusion is especially high when the death penalty is at stake. Imagine twelve perfectly nice people who would rather be home watching Dr. Phil suddenly forced to decide a matter of life and death. What helpful advice do they receive? That in deciding whether to impose the death penalty they must consider **aggravating** and **mitigating** circumstances.

The problem, as Professor Tiersma points out, is that the average layman hasn't a clue what the terms "aggravating" and "mitigating" mean in the legal context. An aggravating factor is one that heightens the seriousness of the defendant's crime; for example, a long history of violent crime. At best, most jurors will understand the word "aggravating" in its colloquial sense as "annoying." Murderers do tend to be pretty annoying—does that mean they should all get the death penalty?

Mitigating factors are those that tend to lessen the

defendant's guilt, such as certain mental conditions. The Supreme Court of Georgia confidently asserted that mitigation "is a word of common meaning and usage" and therefore need not be explained to a jury. Try to remember the last time you heard the word "mitigation" used in everyday conversation.

Perplexed jurors will sometimes beg judges to explain such terms as aggravating and mitigating in plain language. Judges, fearful of getting reversed on appeal, typically refuse to deviate from the standard instructions; in fact, many states actually prohibit judges from giving jurors written copies of the instructions. Even where it is allowed, judges are sometimes reluctant to provide hard copies, possibly to avoid a reprimand from a higher court. A recent study of trials in Washington State found that juries asking for clarification of the judge's instructions received such helpful responses as:

> "No additional instructions will be given."
> "Please read the instructions again."
> "You have received all of the instructions . . . no clarification will be provided."

And thank you for doing your civic duty!

A 2004 murder trial in Massachusetts ended with a jury instruction that ran to over fifty pages—even the judge lost her place while reading them. When the jury requested a written copy of the instruction, she declined. It was only after two more days of pleas from the jury that the judge finally relented.

For as long as there have been juries, there has been confusion over jury instructions. Back in 1314, an English jury was asked to decide whether a parcel of land was **free alms** or **lay fee**. The jurors, displaying a woeful ignorance of the law (but an admirable command of the subjunctive) complained to the judge "we be no lawyers." The impatient judge replied, "Good people, say what you think."

Although judges have historically resisted clarifying the law for juries, they are sometimes happy to give their personal opinion as to the credibility of the witnesses. As recently as 1979, a British judge caused a furor by delivering an outrageously pro-defendant jury instruction at the conclusion of the conspiracy trial of politician Jeremy Thorpe. The late Peter Cook brilliantly satirized the incident in a sketch called "Entirely a Matter for You" (reprinted in *Tragically I Was an Only Twin* [2002]), in which the judge blithely remarks:

> We have heard, for example, from Mr. Bex Bissell: a man who by his own admission is a liar, a humbug, a hypocrite, a vagabond, a loathsome spotted reptile and a self-confessed chicken strangler. You may choose, if you wish, to believe the transparent tissue of odious lies which streamed on and on from his disgusting, greedy, slavering lips. That is entirely a matter for you.

In America, jury instructions got off to a promising start. In the early days of the republic, according to legal historian Lawrence Friedman, judges used to speak to juries off the cuff, in frank, commonsense language. As the nineteenth century progressed, however, appellate courts became increasingly keen to reverse the freewheeling lower courts at the slightest hint of legal error. As judges grew more cautious, jury instructions congealed into plodding, wordy documents that set forth the law in abstract terms.

One of the most troublesome phrases for jurors is **reasonable doubt**, as in, "the prosecution must prove the defendant's guilt beyond a reasonable doubt." In 1850, one Massachusetts court tied itself in verbal knots describing reasonable doubt as something "that leaves the minds of the jurors in that condition that they cannot say that they feel an abiding conviction . . . of the truth of the charge."

Come again? Never mind the double negatives and the obscure use of "abiding conviction," this formulation was such a hit with the profession that it was ultimately inserted into the California Penal Code in 1929. The very same language found its way into Judge Ito's jury instruction in the 1995 O. J. Simpson trial. Small wonder prosecutors in that case were unable to secure a conviction, abiding or otherwise.

Occasionally, courts pooh-pooh jury instructions on the grounds that legal concepts such as reasonable doubt are indefinable. In 1889 a Mississippi court declined to reverse a murder conviction that had been based on an utterly opaque jury instruction, saying "All that can be urged against the [instruction] is that it is another instance of the vain attempt to do the impossible, *i.e.,* to define that indefinable thing, reasonable doubt." Of course, one sympathizes with any judge asked to put the *je ne sais quoi* of reasonable doubt into words, but still, it might be worth the effort.

Jury instructions desperately need help from the Plain English brigade. In 1997, California's Judicial Council took up the challenge of reforming both its criminal and civil jury instructions with the radical goal of making them understandable for the average juror.

The Judicial Council enthusiastically followed the principles of plain English—using active voice, avoiding double negatives, and writing shorter sentences (Peter Tiersma is one of their consultants). In August 2005, the new criminal instructions were approved.

Efforts such as these have met resistance from—now here's a shocker—the Precision School. Professor David Crump, whom we last met in Chapter 2 defending "the party of the first part," argues that "accuracy is at a premium in jury instructions. It cannot be sacrificed for plainness." Which assumes that any increase in "plainness" will be at the expense of "accuracy"—a false dichotomy if ever there was. Consider the following comparison of old and new California jury instructions:

> **OLD:** Failure of recollection is common. Innocent misrecollection is not uncommon.
> **NEW:** People often forget things or make mistakes in what they remember.
> **OLD:** Direct evidence is evidence that directly proves a fact. It is evidence which by itself, if found to be true, establishes that fact. Circumstantial evidence is evidence that, if found to be true, proves a fact from which an inference of the existence of another fact may be drawn. An inference is a deduction of fact that may logically and reasonably be drawn from another fact or group of facts established by the evidence.
> **NEW:** [I]f a witness testifies he saw it raining outside before he came into the courthouse, that testimony is direct evidence that it was raining. . . . [I]f a witness testifies that he saw someone come

inside wearing a raincoat covered with drops of water, that testimony is circumstantial evidence because it may support a conclusion that it was raining outside.

Across the pond, the British judiciary has gotten into the act, drafting jury instructions that sound dangerously sensible. Remember all the existential angst expressed by judges who could not put "reasonable doubt" into words? Well, here's how a British judge would now explain it to a jury:

How does the prosecution succeed in proving the defendant's guilt? The answer is—by making you sure of it. Nothing less than that will do. If after considering all the evidence you are sure that the defendant is guilty, you must return a verdict of 'Guilty.' If you are not sure, your verdict must be 'Not Guilty.'

There—was that so hard?

Despite their heroic efforts, juries sometimes fail to reach any decision at all. This is known as a **hung jury**, and according to recent statistics, it happens about eight thousand times a year in the United States.

A hung jury has nothing to do with a **hanging judge**. In fact, it's quite the reverse, since a hung jury can't make up its mind, while a hanging judge is thought to be a little too eager to make up his. The *Oxford English Dictionary* lists the first printed reference to a hung jury in Edwin Bryant's *What I Saw in California* (1848–49), in which he states: "The jury . . . were what is called 'hung'; they could not agree. . . ."

Bryant's phrasing suggests that the phrase was already in common use by the late 1840s. Indeed, there are earlier case reports—generally from southern states—with references to hung jury and variations thereof. The earliest recorded use of the term is in an 1821 Kentucky case, *Evans v. McKinsey*. So it appears that "hung jury" developed in the American South during the early nineteenth century.

Incidentally, the term **jury-rigged**, meaning assembled in a makeshift manner, has nothing to do with the legal sense of the word jury. It is an eighteenth-century nautical term, deriving from the Latin *adjutare* (to aid), from which we also get the military word "adjutant."

MANY A QUAINT AND CURIOUS VOLUME

When all is said and done, the result of litigation—apart from some very satisfied lawyers—is a written decision. Judicial decisions are published in books called **law reports**—volume after volume after volume. When you see a lawyer on TV against a backdrop of official-looking books, they're probably law reports. Because everything in Anglo-American law depends on precedent, law reports are the single greatest authority as to our rights and responsibilities. They represent the distilled wisdom of centuries of judicial thought.

On the whole, they make lousy reading. They are as wordy, technical, and dry as one would expect from hundreds of pages of densely packed legalese. And erudite— judges are learned men and women, and they won't let you forget it. In one 1997 opinion, for example, a federal judge reminds us that **laches**—the argument that a plaintiff delayed too long in filing a lawsuit—"is an equitable defense based on the maxim *vigilantibus non dormientibus aequitas subvenit*" and then immediately provides the English equivalent: "equity aids the vigilant, not those who sleep on their rights." The real translation being, "Look at me, I speak Latin!"

And yet, now and again, one comes across a decision worth reading. Judge Bruce Selya, for example, likes to poke fun at lawyers' obsession with citing authority for every proposition by peppering his opinions with lines like "But appearances can be deceiving. *See* Aesop, *The Wolf in Sheep's Clothing* (Circa 550 B.C.)" British judges sometimes display a certain literary flair, and none of them more so than the late Lord Denning (1899–1999). In case after case, Denning distinguished himself from the run-of-the-mill judges with his whimsical style:

> In summertime, village cricket is a delight to everyone. Nearly every village has its own cricket field where the young men play and the old men watch. In the village of Lintz in the County of Durham they have their own ground, where they have played these last 70 years. They tend it well. The wicket area is well rolled and mown. . . .

Denning's opening lines often left no doubt as to where his sympathies lay:

> To some this may appear to be a small matter, but to Mr. Harry Hook, it is very important. He is a street trader in the Barnsley Market. He has been trading there for some six years without any complaint

being made against him; but, nevertheless, he has now been banned from trading in the market for life. All because of a trifling incident . . .

In one case, a parking lot operator punctiliously argued that a customer should have read the conditions printed on the back of the parking lot ticket (the one that the machine spits out). Denning breezily rejected the argument, observing with rare common sense, "No customer in a thousand ever read the conditions [on the back of a parking lot ticket]. If he had stopped to do so, he would have missed the train or the boat."

If you hunt through the law reports you'll even find poetry. In 1983, for example, a Michigan court faced an utterly frivolous lawsuit brought on behalf of a tree that had been hit by a car. The judges dismissed the suit with nothing more than twelve lines of original verse modeled on Joyce Kilmer's famous poem "Trees." It began:

> We thought that we would never see
> A suit to compensate a tree.

In 2002, Pennsylvania judge J. Michael Eakin used poetry to support the petition of a woman who wanted to invalidate her prenuptial agreement. The reason? Her husband—a much older man, and a millionaire to boot—had given her a "diamond" ring that turned out to be a fake. Judge Eakin waxed poetic:

> A groom must expect matrimonial pandemonium
> when his spouse finds he's given her a cubic zirconium. . . .
> She was 19, he was nearly 30 years older;

was it unreasonable for her to believe what he told her?
Given their history and Pygmalion relation,
I find her reliance was with justification.
Given his accomplishment and given her youth,
Was it unjustifiable for her to think he told the truth?
Or for every prenuptial is it now a must,
that you treat your betrothed with presumptive mistrust?

Not only was Eakin overruled by the other two judges on the panel, but his killjoy brethren even went out of their way to express "grave concern" that the use of rhyme "reflects poorly on the Supreme Court of Pennsylvania."

Lighten up. Eakin's bit of doggerel is nothing compared to that of a Kansas judge who once sentenced a prostitute to prison with an opinion that began with this couplet:

On January 30th, nineteen seventy-four,
This lass agreed to work as a whore.

For that, the judge earned an official reprimand from the Kansas Supreme Court.

If you find yourself developing a taste for law reports—and, like soap operas, they can be addictive despite the long stretches of tedium—the future has never looked brighter. Litigation is one of America's great growth industries, promising an ever-increasing flow of court decisions. The inexorable growth of lawsuits in the United States is mainly due to an area of the law called **tort**, which we will examine in the next chapter.

4

ANY TORT IN A STORM

*[T]he plaintiff alleged that the defendant had slandered him by saying **Thou art as arrant a thief as any is in England;** . . . The plea was held bad because the plaintiff had failed to allege (or prove) that there were any thieves in England; if there were none, the statement was obviously not defamatory!*

— PETER M. TIERSMA, *LEGAL LANGUAGE* (1999),
CITING *FOSTER* V. *BROWNING* (1625)

N ext time you get the urge to do a good deed, consider the fate of Taylor Ostergaard and Lindsey Zellitti.

Taylor and Lindsey were two teenage girls in Durango, Colorado. One evening in July 2004, they decided to skip the high school dance. Instead, they baked chocolate chip cookies and left them as presents for various neighbors. They even delivered each batch of cookies with a heart-shaped note saying "Have a Great Evening."

Shortly after 10 P.M., the girls dropped off some cookies at the home of Wanita Young, a forty-nine-year-old cashier at the local Wal-Mart. Ms. Young, unfortunately, had what one might charitably call a high-strung disposition. She allegedly mistook the gentle knocks at her door to be those of a craven (but oddly polite) burglar. Ms. Young ended up in the emergency room with an anxiety attack.

Although Taylor and Lindsey apologized and offered to pay any medical bills, Ms. Young took the girls to court. On February 3, 2005, Judge Doug Walker of the La Plata County Small Claims Court ordered the girls to pay $900 for Ms. Young's medical expenses. The judge did, however, turn down Ms. Young's request for $3,000 in additional damages, including "lost wages."

The branch of law that allows people like Wanita Young to sue their neighbors for random acts of kindness is called **tort**. Indeed, a lawyer might even say that Ms. Young's suit created a whole new tort: negligent delivery of cookies.

Tort is one of those words that mystifies nonlawyers.

Unlike terms such as "evidence" or "jury", "tort" has never found its way into ordinary conversation. And yet, tort is all around us. The lawsuits that make headlines— asbestos, tobacco, McDonald's coffee—are based on tort. Politicians blather on about "tort reform" assuming that people know what tort is and why it might be in need of reform.

Let me explain. A tort is any wrongful act by one person that gives another person the right to sue him or her. If that sounds broad, it's because it is. In fact, to call tort a broad term is a serious understatement: tort is the law's catchall category, a vast legal piñata stuffed with consolation prizes for your better sort of victim. Personal injury, emotional distress, and cookie-induced hysteria: These and many other maladies are the subject of tort law.

TWIST AND SUE

As far as legal language goes, tort law has generated dozens of terms seemingly designed to confound lovers of plain English. For starters, there's tort itself, which isn't even an English word.

Tort is an old French word meaning "injury." It comes from the Latin verb *torquere* (to twist), from which we get such useful words as torque and torsion. In case you were wondering, the word is wholly unrelated to the pastry known as a torte, which comes from the Latin *torta* (flat cake).

English lawyers first began using tort to refer to non-contractual liability as early as 1586, but the word was not particularly popular at first. Sir William Blackstone (1723–80), whose four-volume treatise *Commentaries on the*

Laws of England covers the entire common law of England, makes no mention of it. Instead, he refers to **private wrongs** and **civil injuries**, both of which phrases, when you think about it, are considerably more descriptive than "tort."

Despite Blackstone's preference for English, lawyers soon veered off into foreign tongues when describing civil wrongs, initially opting for *delictum,* an ancient Roman legal term. Anglicized into **delict**, the word is now hopelessly old-fashioned, but it is still a valid legal term that can be found in countless dictionaries.

More recognizably, delict survives in the phrase *in flagrante delicto*. Most people translate this as "caught having sex," but that is a later spin on the Latin. Literally it means "[caught] while the offense is flaming." This is a noticeably handy term for the law—various courts have used it, both in its generic and sexual senses—but it does not appear in statutes or law dictionaries. Except in Iraq, that is, where the Interim Constitution provided that members of the National Assembly have immunity from any criminal prosecution unless they are caught "*in flagrante delicto.*" No wonder it took them so long to form a government.

It was only in the nineteenth century that the word "tort" came into its own. The first English-language book on the subject was written in 1859 by a Boston lawyer named Francis Hilliard. The cover page rather boldly announces *The Law of Torts* and then, in slightly smaller print, *Or Private Wrongs.* Even twenty years later, when the American jurist Thomas Cooley published his *Treatise on the Law of Torts,* he was obliged to add the explanatory subtitle, *Or, The Wrongs Which Arise Independent of Contract*. By the early twentieth century, however, tort had become the universally acknowledged term for this branch of the law.

Which is all well and good, but doesn't answer the question of why the legal profession would abandon perfectly good English phrases like "private wrongs" and "civil injuries" in favor of an archaic French word. Not even the French use the word *tort* as a legal term; they say *la responsabilité extracontractuelle*.

Does the Precision School have an answer? The one thing they could possibly say in defense of tort is that it takes up only four letters, but that's pretty pathetic. After all, *mort* is an equally brief French word, but in English we splurge on the extra letter and write "death," even in legal documents.

Besides being obscure, the word "tort" has spawned some truly grotesque offspring, including **tortious** and **tortfeasor**, the latter being "a person who commits a tort." Tortfeasor doesn't even look like a real word but trust me, you will find it in any English-language law dictionary. The "feasor" part, incidentally, also comes from a French verb—*faire* (to do).

Tortfeasor, in turn, gives rise to such disturbing formulations as the **phantom tortfeasor** defense. This defense arose in a 1998 Tennessee case against Wal-Mart (Wal-Mart crops up a lot where lawsuits are concerned) in which a young boy slipped on some ice cubes left in a store aisle. Wal-Mart argued that the ice cubes were left not by one of its employees but rather by some unknown third party, to whom they gave the exotic moniker "the phantom tortfeasor."

The phantom tortfeasor theory, although legally untenable, at least has the virtue of being one of the very few law terms that can be turned into a comic book character:

> "Mr. President, I'm afraid there's been another unexplained spill at Wal-Mart."
>
> "Wal-Mart? Where was Wanita?"
>
> "She was out with an anxiety attack."
>
> "Dammit, Colonel, tell me exactly what happened."
>
> "You're not going to like this sir: ice cubes, lawsuits . . ."
>
> "Dear God, not the Phantom Tortfeasor! Wait a second, is that a knock at the door? Who could be delivering cookies at this hour?"

Wal-Mart lost the case. The court insisted that the store produce evidence that the mysterious wrongdoer actually existed—which would have made their tortfeasor distinctly less phantomlike.

IT'S THE THOUGHT
THAT COUNTS

In the old days, tort law was concerned exclusively with intentional acts—that is, you could only sue another person if that person had purposely set out to do you harm. Mere accidents didn't cut it. The original tort lawsuit carried the highly descriptive label of **trespass vi et armis** ("trespass by force and arms"). Trespass here does not refer to wandering onto somebody else's land, but more generally to a transgression. This early sense of the word still survives in most translations of the Lord's Prayer— "forgive us our trespasses as we forgive those who trespass against us."

The most infamous intentional tort is **battery**, as in "assault and battery." The word comes from the Latin *bauttere* (to beat) and is related to battering and battle. Benjamin Franklin was the first to use the word to describe an electrical cell in 1748; it is thought that he did so because the contraption could discharge jolts of electricity, much like a "battery" of artillery.

Battery often entails "beating up" another person, but from the law's perspective, *any* unauthorized touching of another person constitutes a battery, even if you don't give the other chap a jolly good thrashing. This is why doctors are so careful about getting you to sign consent forms before surgery. Without your consent, virtually every medical procedure would constitute a common law battery.

But wait—you might be thinking—*isn't battery a crime?* Yes, it is (see Chapter 6), but then it's not unusual that one act can lead to both a criminal prosecution and a private lawsuit. That is why O. J. Simpson could famously be acquitted for the *crime* of homicide but then be privately sued for the *tort* of wrongful death.

OOPS!
NEGLIGENCE

Had tort law confined itself to intentional acts, it would be a mere shadow of its current self. The massive growth in tort law has to do with liability for unintentional, or **negligent**, acts.

The word "negligence" entered the law sideways as a Latin adverb (*negligenter*) used to describe a kind of trespass that was *not* done with "force and arms." Blackstone recognized a whole category of unintentional civil wrongs, including the unskillful work of a "physician, surgeon, or apothecary," which he called **mala praxis**, from Latin *malum* (bad) plus Greek *praxis* (practice)—the forerunner of **malpractice**.

This was the stuff of negligence, but Blackstone did not use that term. Lawsuits for damages caused by unintentional acts were seen as exceptional cases. Lawyers had to bring them as actions for **trespass on the case**, which was a shorthand way of asking the court to make an exception to the doctrine of trespass (i.e., intentional torts) on the facts of the particular case.

Despite the existence of this special procedure, many English lawyers viewed the prospect of suing someone for a trespass that did not actually involve force and arms as vaguely suspicious, if not downright unsporting. The seventeenth-century lawyer John Cowell, who you may recall gave us "hoghenhine" and "ale-tastor," distrusted the notion that you could have a trespass without a bit of grievous bodily harm to go with it. In his dictionary, Cowell would only go so far as to observe, somewhat tentatively, that there was a species of trespass that "seemeth to be without force." Even in the early twentieth century, New Zealand Solicitor General Sir John Salmond could stoutly deny the existence of a tort of negligence, although by then such a position was a little eccentric.

Long story short: Negligence has come to mean any action so stupid that it violates a "duty of care" that we owe one another. The only fly in the ointment is that there has never been a clear definition of exactly what our "duty of care" entails; courts make it up as they go along.

As a result, new forms of negligence blossom like tulips in the spring. *Black's Law Dictionary* lists no fewer than seventeen varieties of negligence, some of them distinguished by exceedingly fine shades of meaning. There is **slight** negligence and **ordinary** negligence; **gross** negligence and **reckless** negligence; **active** negligence and **imputed** negligence; and even the seemingly contradictory **willful** negligence, which describes the act of intentionally doing something by accident.

Although it defies logic, the term "willful negligence" appears in federal environmental laws, as well as in countless form contracts, such as the boilerplate lease that exempts the landlord from liability, "except for acts of gross negligence or willful negligence." Judges, who are routinely called upon to interpret this phrase, have wearily tried to explain its absurdity. In 1983, one federal appellate judge wrote that willful negligence "makes as much sense as 'guilty innocence.'"

There is serious money to be made in negligence law. New York City alone paid out $570 million in negligence awards in 2004; private corporations pay out much more. It is notoriously difficult to calculate the aggregate cost of America's tort system. One study estimates the annual cost in 2006 at $295 billion—by an intriguing coincidence, just about the annual revenue of Wal-Mart. It's no wonder politicians speak of **tort reform**—that is, legislation to deter tort lawsuits.

Tens of thousands of plaintiffs' lawyers stand ready to take on your negligence case for a **contingency fee**—if they win, they take 30 to 40 percent of the money, but if they lose, they get nothing. Their tort theories are nothing if not creative. In a 1999 lawsuit, plaintiffs' lawyers tried to establish the tort of "toothbrush abrasion," which was allegedly caused by "unsafe and unreasonably dangerous" toothbrushes. It makes one bristle.

BE *REASONABLE,* DEAR! OR, WHEN BAD THINGS HAPPEN TO MEN IN CLAPHAM

Arguably the person most responsible for the emergence of negligence as a separate tort was not a judge or even a lawyer, but an engineer, John Loudon McAdam. In the early 1800s, McAdam pioneered a new method of road construction that vastly improved the British turnpike system. Improved roads led to a great increase in the traffic of stagecoaches, all of them vying for the fastest travel time, and many of them ending up in horrendous accidents. The result was a glut of lawsuits seeking remedies for what were the inevitable, though unintended, results of the drivers' haste.

Incidentally, roads built by the McAdam system are said to be "macadamized"; and when somebody thought of covering such roads with tar, the result was tar-bound macadam, or **tarmac**.

By the 1830s it was settled that all those people injured on macadamized roads could sue for damages caused by the drivers' negligence without having to shoehorn their lawsuits into the "trespass" doctrine. This legal innovation came just in time for the Industrial Revolution, which gave mankind spectacular new ways to behave negligently. The railroads alone killed or injured more than twenty thousand workers in the United States during 1888–89—a rate that would double by 1906. Under these conditions, according to Lawrence Friedman, the locomotive was developing tort law "on its own steam."

Even hidebound courts recognized that at least some industrial injuries deserved compensation, and they struggled to define the "duty of care" in language that was sufficiently elastic to cope with a changing world. In 1856, one English court came up with the so-called **reasonable man** standard that remains the test for negligence today. According to this standard, negligence amounts to doing something (or failing to do something) that a reasonable man would not have done (or would have done) under the same circumstances.

Sounds good, doesn't it? Who doesn't want to be reasonable? And surely a person who acts negligently is being *un*reasonable. But try, just try, to get twelve people to agree on what is reasonable in a given situation. There is no scientific definition to rely on; dictionaries define "reasonable" by reference to other equally vague terms, such as "sensible," "sane," and "rational." Lawyers, however, bandy the word about to an extent that is almost, well, unreasonable. Not only in the context of the "reasonable man," but also in such phrases as **reasonable doubt**—and we saw in Chapter 3 how much trouble those two words can cause.

Reasonable is a classic example of the law's use of language that is—to put it politely—deliberately flexible. Other examples include **substantial** and **satisfactory**. These are weasel words. They evade the messy details and give lawyers free rein to interpret as the occasion demands.

The reasonable man—and kindred legal expressions— ought to be more nails in the coffin of the Precision School.

Who could claim that legalese is precise when it depends on words as malleable as Silly Putty? No matter, many lawyers consider the reasonable man, or **reasonable person**, standard not only to be clear, but they seriously refer to it as the **objective test** of negligence, despite the fact that it is as subjective as the day is long. Reasonableness is in the eye of the beholder.

To illustrate the point, let's return to our theme and ask: Who *is* the reasonable person of negligence law? Some judges read "reasonable" to mean "average." In 1903, an English judge, Lord Bowen, memorably described the reasonable person as **the man on the Clapham omnibus**; in other words, your everyday middle-class Londoner. Another judge described him as "the man who takes the magazines at home and in the evening pushes the lawn mower in his shirt sleeves." Again, this is meant to portray a soothing image of the average Joe (unless of course the magazine is *Gun Nut Weekly* and he's pushing the lawn mower over his wife).

More typically, courts define the reasonable person not as an average being, but as a model citizen who embodies the qualities that society—that is, the judge—considers to be "reasonable." Over time, it has become increasingly clear that this reasonable man, whoever he may be, reads the backs of parking tickets and is not the sort of person whom you want at your next party. As A. P. Herbert writes in his legal spoof, *Uncommon Law* (1937):

> The Reasonable Man is always thinking of others; prudence is his guide and "Safety First" . . . is his rule of life. He is one who invariably looks where he is going . . . and will inform himself of the history

and habits of a dog before administering a caress . . . who in the way of business looks only for that margin of profit which twelve men such as himself would reckon to be "fair" . . . who uses nothing except in moderation and even while he flogs his children is meditating only on the golden mean.

Skilled lawyers used the very flexibility of the "reasonable man" to expand the frontiers of negligence just as quickly as modern machines could mangle their clients. That led to a judicial backlash. In 1931, Chief Justice Benjamin Cardozo warned against opening "the floodgates of litigation," a phrase that has since become synonymous with tort law run amok. It's often assumed that Cardozo coined the floodgates metaphor, but the expression had already been in use for over a century when he said it. The first recorded use of "the floodgates of litigation" is a New York case, *Whitbeck* v. *Cook* (1818).

Incidentally, the Precision School likes to think of itself as the guardian of those floodgates, even while they turn a blind eye to litigation-producing words like "reasonable." In a 1987 article, a retired lawyer named Edmund Righter trotted out the floodgates metaphor to argue against substituting plain English for legalese. The thing that really ticked him off was another lawyer's suggestion that it would be acceptable to write "due" rather than "due and payable." If lawyers start doing that, Righter warned, "you will open up the floodgates of litigation."

Tort litigation ends up with a finding of **liability**— essentially, blame. This is an awkward subject for polite conversation and it tends to make judges break out into fits of nervous Latin. In the Victorian era, courts became inordinately fond of the phrase *volenti non fit injuria:* You can't sue for injury if you voluntarily assumed the risk. This doctrine made it easy for judges to shield large industrial concerns from liability—after all, every factory worker "voluntarily" exposes himself to danger by coming to work. I suppose one can forgive judges for knowing which side their bread was buttered on—but not for using Latin when a perfectly good English expression was at hand, namely "assumption of risk."

At the same time *volenti* was taking flight, more plaintiff-friendly courts invented a doctrine that allows an injured person to win compensation even when he can't prove negligence: *res ipsa loquitur.* The concept arose in the British case of *Byrne* v. *Boadle* (1863). In that case, Mr. Byrne was walking past Mr. Boadle's warehouse when a barrel of flour fell on his head. Byrne had no direct evidence that the falling barrel was caused by Boadle's negligence, but the judge, Lord Pollock, reasoned that the falling barrel "spoke for itself," that is, barrels don't just fall out of warehouses unless somebody was negligent.

Unsatisfied with the sound of "the thing speaks for itself," Lord Pollock rummaged around his bag of Latin tricks and borrowed a phrase from Cicero which means exactly the same thing—*res ipsa loquitur.*

Despite the obvious charms of speaking Latin, there is no reason why lawyers today need to follow Lord Pollock in referring to *res ipsa loquitur*—one could use, for example, English. Nonetheless, lawyers are addicted to the Latin phrase; the great enablers of that addiction are members of the Precision School. In his 1960 article,

"Let's Not Oversimplify Legal Language," former Marquette Law School professor Ray Aiken defended *res ipsa* on the basis that there was no decent English alternative. "I would feel a bit foolish," wrote Aiken, "attempting to instruct my classes upon the doctrine of 'the thing speaks for itself.'"

Aiken's self-defeating argument assumes that word-for-word translation is the only way to convert a foreign phrase into English, which is nonsense, as any Frenchman who has ever tried to have a head-to-head conversation will tell you. One could recast *res ipsa loquitur* into any number of English phrases, such as **self-evident negligence** or **presumed negligence**.

Although using English is a step in the right direction, not all English is plain. There are, for example, the confusing fraternal twins **comparative negligence** and **contributory negligence**. Comparative negligence, which is the rule in most American states, means that if a person's injury was partly caused by his own carelessness, then he is not entitled to 100 percent of the compensation. Instead, the court will reduce the plaintiff's compensation by a certain percentage—if he was 50 percent negligent, then he gets only 50 percent of the money.

If you are unlucky enough to live in a state that hasn't embraced comparative negligence, then you're subject to the law of contributory negligence. Under that rule, if the injured party was even a little bit careless, then his compensation is reduced, not by a percentage, but all the way to zero. To say the least, contributory negligence is a harsh doctrine. In one nineteenth-century case, the family of a four-year-old boy killed by a speeding train sued the railroad for negligence. The court held that the railroad—even if it had been negligent—had no obligation to compensate the family since the boy had also been negligent in walking so near the tracks. In a Minnesota case, a manufacturer whose supply of flax was destroyed by sparks from a nearby train could not recover its losses from the railroad. The damage was at least partially due to the manufacturer's negligence in storing his flax so close to a rail yard. With depressing regularity, people who sued railroad companies were told that they had been guilty of contributory negligence.

Courts began to reject contributory negligence in favor of comparative negligence in the 1940s—interestingly, just about the time when the railroad lost its preeminent position as a mode of transportation. Today, Britain and all but five American states have abolished contributory negligence.

If you win a negligence lawsuit, you will end up with **damages**, which sounds bad—haven't you suffered enough already?—but that is just the law's illogical way of referring to "compensation for the damage you suffered." Why not just call it "compensation"? Incidentally, the law will compensate you for your broken bones even if you happen to have unusually brittle bones. After all, the brittle bones are not your fault, so there's no comparative negligence to reduce your damages. This rule—"a tortfeasor takes his victim as he finds him"—is universally known among lawyers by the cringe-inducing name **the eggshell skull doctrine**.

The eggshell skull doctrine can be traced to a 1901 English case (*Dulieu* v. *White & Sons*) that, oddly enough, had nothing to do with skull injuries. Rather, it concerned a pregnant woman, Mrs. Dulieu, who had been tending bar in her husband's pub when a horse-drawn van plowed through the wall of the pub, nearly running her down. Not surprisingly, the incident sent Mrs. Dulieu into shock and caused her to give birth prematurely.

Although neither mother nor child suffered any physical harm, Mrs. Dulieu sued the owner of the van, White & Sons, for causing her "nervous shock." White & Sons argued that they should only be liable for damage that was the **reasonably foreseeable** outcome of their driver's action—and who could have foreseen that there would be an emotionally fragile pregnant woman inside the pub? The case came up for trial before Mr. Justice Kennedy of the Court of King's Bench, who sided with Mrs. Dulieu. It was foreseeable that *somebody* would be inside the pub, according to the judge, and the fact that that person turned out to be unusually susceptible to shock was the defendant's problem.

Kennedy explained his reasoning by way of some hypothetical examples: "It is no answer to the sufferer's claim for damages that he would have suffered less injury, or no injury at all, if he had not had an unusually thin skull or an unusually weak heart." Later commentators evidently found the "thin skull" example to be more memorable than the real facts of the case which is why, sadly, the rule that a tortfeasor takes his victim as he finds him is not known as the **pregnant barmaid rule**.

The decision in *Dulieu* is famous for another reason: It was the first case to allow a plaintiff to recover damages for **psychiatric injury**. This precedent paved the way for lawsuits concerning every type of mental wound, from Post-Traumatic Stress Disorder to Wanita Young's cookie-phobia.

NIMBY-PIMBY

After this un-plain talk, a breath of fresh air comes from a branch of tort that is concerned, among other things, with bad smells.

Let's say your neighbors—and I think you know which ones I mean—are total slobs. They throw garbage into their yard and let it rot; their dogs relieve themselves around the house; they stay up till all hours listening to AC/DC at full blast; and oh, yes, they're adding a micro-brewery to their property.

These people are a **nuisance**, and that is exactly what the law calls them. The word comes from the Latin *nocere* (to hurt), from which we get such related words as "annoy-ance," "noise," and "noxious." You can't get much plainer than that.

All sorts of human activities can amount to nuisance, even activities that appear to be socially acceptable. In February 2006, for example, a Rhode Island court held that three paint companies had created a "public nuisance" by selling lead paint in the 1960s and '70s—*before* there was any ban on lead paint. Although a nuisance is ordinar-ily something repellent, it can sometimes be positively inviting. If a child's curiosity leads him onto a property with open manholes, dangerous fumes, or other irresistible hazards, the parents can sue the property owner for creat-ing an **attractive nuisance**—and they can throw in a claim for willful negligence while they're at it.

As a legal concept, nuisance arose to fill a gap in medieval property law: There was no remedy for situations where your neighbor managed to harm your property without leaving his own. The law knew what to do when somebody trespassed on your property or physically attacked you or dispossessed you of your land. But the law was helpless against your slovenly, AC/DC-loving neighbors. That is, until sometime around the thirteenth century, when common law courts began to recognize a procedure known as the **assize of nuisance**—basically, the nuisance-makers would have to turn down the music or pay you money.

Nuisance was a fairly limited doctrine at first; in an age when farm animals roamed freely in and out of houses, how much could one complain? It became a larger issue in the sixteenth and seventeenth centuries with the growth of towns and certain trades. Leading court cases from this period involved the decidedly pungent smells emanating from tanneries, breweries, and chandlers (candle makers).

It is interesting to note that English judges probably never would have intervened in any of these cases had they thought that bad smells were merely unpleasant. These were sturdy folk who didn't have much patience for fussy plaintiffs. At the time, however, medical science held that bad smells carried diseases, making nuisance a matter of public health rather than merely private taste. The smell theory of disease—known as the **miasma theory**—remained prevalent until the mid-nineteenth century and counted among its adherents the Crimean War nurse Florence Nightingale. "Miasma" (the Greek word for "pollution") is not, of course, a legal term, but it is interesting all the same.

Smell is not the only nuisance. Even if your neighbor is scrupulously fragrant, he or she might put up a building that blocks your natural light, or spoils your view, or is just plain ugly. That sort of thing can also be a legal nuisance. Thus, a 1901 treatise defines nuisance as "any offensive erection." Including, presumably, one that lasts more than four hours.

And music can be deemed a nuisance, even if it isn't AC/DC. In 1956, a justice of the Pennsylvania Supreme Court held that a jukebox offering only jazz records met the definition of "nuisance." Jazz, he said,

> robs the air of sweet silence, it substitutes for the gentle concord of stillness the wailings of the so-called "blues singer," the whining of foggy saxophones, the screeching of untuned fiddles, the blast of head-splitting horns, and the battering of ear-shattering drums. It makes a mockery of music. . . .

Hard to believe that there was a time when the most obnoxious music that a judge could shake his fist at was jazz. Makes one nostalgic, doesn't it? In any event, the judge was overruled by his brethren; the jukebox was allowed to go on screeching for the benefit of those crazy kids with their bobby sox and ginger ale. After all, the proprietors of restaurants, diners, and the like had to make a living too.

That's the thing about nuisance law; it is a never-ending struggle to balance the public's right to enjoy their property on the one hand, and the utility of certain—even smelly or noisy—trades on the other. As long ago as 1605, an English court refused to allow a nuisance claim against a candle maker because, as the judge said with a delightful show of legal franglais, "L'utilité de la chose excuse le noisomeness de la stink." Twenty-three years later, another judge defended tanners in similarly Clouseau-like language: "Un tan-house est necessary car touts wear shoes" ("a tan-house is necessary because everyone wears shoes").

These people have to ply their trade somewhere. True, says the plaintiff, but not *here*. Not surprisingly, nuisance lawsuits are sometimes referred to as **NIMBY** (not in my back yard) lawsuits. One of the most famous NIMBY lawsuits in recent years involved a scheme to build electricity-generating wind turbines in the waters between Cape Cod and Martha's Vineyard. The lawsuit to stop the project attracted the enthusiastic support of people who normally extol the virtues of renewable energy—Ted Kennedy and Walter Cronkite, to name two—but who also happen to have summer houses in view of the planned windmills.

It should be noted that for every resident NIMBY, there's usually a PIMBY (put it in my back yard): This is the guy who stands to benefit from the construction of, say, a prison or a nuclear power plant. One creative blogger even suggested that a PIMBY culture could be created by requiring utilities to give preferential pricing to anyone who lives within sight of a generating plant. An appealing thought, but it will probably be some time before one sees ads for a "three-bedroom colonial, full view of cooling towers."

The law comes to the aid of potential NIMBY plaintiffs by protecting property owners' rights to enjoy amenities such as light and air. These rights came to be known as **easements**, a word that took a tortured path to law by way of the French *aisement,* meaning toilet, or going to the toilet. Even after the word was adopted into English, it initially retained its connection to privies—a 1586 military ordinance, for example, orders imprisonment for any soldier caught doing his "easement" except "as in such places as is appointed for that purpose." In plain English, this refers to Number Twosies.

McLIBEL: OVER A BILLION SERVED

One final branch of tort deserves mention for its confusing terminology. That is **defamation**, which is the law concerning insults of one sort or another. Defamation comes from the Old French *disfame,* or dishonor; more familiar words are **libel** and **slander**, which both refer to communications that hurt a person's reputation.

"Slander" derives from the same Latin root as "scandal." The connection is no coincidence. Originally, a slander had to be pretty scandalous to get you into court: generally, something along the lines of accusing somebody of committing a felony or imputing "unchastity" to a woman. Or disease. Early slander law got much of its oomph from the seventeenth-century fashion of accusing one's rivals of having "the pox." Pox was code for syphilis, otherwise known as the "French pox."

Although there hasn't been a pox lawsuit lately, in 1996 a Harlem schoolteacher named Daria Carter-Clark sued the writer Joe Klein for "imputing unchastity" to her, which, in New York State, is still a valid basis for a slander suit. The alleged act of unchastity was having sex with Bill Clinton. Klein's best-selling novel *Primary Colors* does, in fact, portray a Southern governor who has a fling with a Harlem teacher who Carter-Clark insists is based on her.

Carter-Clark even tried to subpoena the president to testify under oath that he never had sex with her (take a number, Daria). Before that testimony could take place, however, the court dismissed the lawsuit. After all, said the court, *Primary Colors* is a work of fiction, even if inspired by real life.

One's good name is as important as good health, or at least it used to be. In the earliest days of colonial America, when survival was a daily struggle, people still took time to sue each other for slander. A Rhode Island code of 1647 catalogs the words that may constitute slander, including **whore**, **whoremaster**, and **cutpurse** (an early name for pickpocket). Presumably the colonial lawmakers would not have gone to the trouble of spelling this out unless there had been a demand for it.

Even when the inflammatory words were spoken, courts were traditionally reluctant to award damages for defamation, based, as legal historian J. H. Baker observes, on "the deep-rooted feeling that mere words were not as serious as sticks and stones."

One way in which courts discouraged defamation cases was the doctrine of *mittior sensus*, a Latin term meaning that a court is obliged to interpret allegedly slanderous words in "the mildest sense" possible. This rule lead to some absolute howlers. In a 1607 case, Sir Thomas Holt sued a man named Astgrigg who had publicly accused Holt of splitting his cook's head in two, so that "one part lay on one shoulder, and another part on the other." The court held that the accusation was not slanderous—after all, the cook might have survived.

In another case from the same year, a certain Lady Morrison sued a man who had boasted that "he hath had the use of the Lady Morrison's body at his pleasure." The defense lawyer argued that the words should be understood in their mildest sense as meaning "to have the use of her body as a tailor, in measuring." Except that the defendant wasn't a tailor—he was a justice of the peace. Lady Morrison won the case.

Although it sounds like an ancient relic, the "mildest sense" doctrine has actually survived for hundreds of years. A 1922 American law dictionary, for example, contains an entry for the word **slut**, the sole purpose of which is to announce that the word merely means "an untidy woman" and therefore is not to be considered slanderous.

The slut doctrine, as I like to call it, came from an 1888 Illinois case that was not officially overruled by the Illinois Supreme Court until 1996—and even then the court was not unanimous. Justice McMorrow delivered a rousing dissent: "[Slut] is not, as the majority suggests, the functional equivalent of charging plaintiff with having engaged in fornication." Any husband can confirm the wisdom of Justice McMorrow's dissent by calling his wife a slut, and then gently explaining that he merely means that she looks a little untidy this morning.

Slander is not the only doctrine available to the violent, sluttish, or disease-ridden. There is also **libel**. The word, which comes from the Latin *libellus* (little book), was once used interchangeably with slander. In the late seventeenth century, however, courts began defining libel narrowly as a written defamation. This sense of libel comes from the *libelli famosi,* defamatory booklets that were printed by early muckrakers.

Putting words on paper—creating a permanent record that can be circulated to one's boss or in-laws—was thought to be inherently more harmful than speaking. The victim of a mere slander, therefore, has to prove that he lost money (known as **special damages**) as a direct result of the slander, while the victim of a libel has no such burden. The upshot is that you'll be considerably better off in court if your enemies take the time to insult you in writing.

To this day, English-speaking countries distinguish between libel and slander, and have even added a third category of defamation: **slander per se**. This refers to certain forms of slander that are so egregious that the plaintiff does *not* have to prove special damages. These include such archaic categories as the imputation of a **loathsome disease** (a phrase that is still dutifully memorized by thousands of bar exam candidates). "Loathsome disease" originally referred to our old friend "the pox" but has now come to include AIDS as well.

The labels attached to different types of defamation—the sort of thing that warms the hearts of Precision-minded lawyers—appear increasingly arbitrary in light of current technology. A statement that constitutes slander per se when spoken, for example, might be tagged **libel per se** if repeated over a broadcast medium. And now, with text, audio, and video streaming over the Internet, maintaining the distinction between libel and slander is utterly pointless. Legal academics get positively giddy over articles with titles like "Should Audio-Visual Defamation on the Internet be Treated as Libel or Slander?" The answer, according to that author, is that "the final determination should be decided as a matter of law, on a case by case basis."

Who cares? If I controlled the Supreme Court—and, frankly, the Court could do a lot worse—there would be only one type of defamation, whether it comes by way of ink, bytes, or an interpretive dance.

But the law goes on creating yet more subcategories of defamation. In recent years, thirteen American states adopted **food disparagement laws**, also known as **veggie libel** laws. These are statutes meant to protect agricultural products—a group with especially tender feelings—from false and disparaging remarks. In 1998, a group of Texas cattlemen sued Oprah Winfrey under the Texas food disparagement law for airing a show about mad cow disease. During the show, Winfrey vowed not to eat another hamburger. A Texas jury rejected the cattlemen's claims.

The Oprah case was a media circus, but it was nothing compared to another food-related defamation case: the **McLibel lawsuit**. That case began in London in 1986 when a group of activists started distributing a pamphlet entitled *What's Wrong with McDonald's: Everything They Don't Want You to Know*. By any standard, the pamphlet was fairly scurrilous, accusing McDonald's of exploiting workers, destroying the South American rain forest, and probably causing gingivitis as well.

McDonald's then made a colossal blunder: It took the activists to court, thus creating the greatest David-and-Goliath struggle the British courts had ever seen. Although two of the defendants settled out with an apology, the other two, Helen Steel and David Morris, decided to fight the case. Poor, with no college education and no lawyers to represent them, Steel and Morris became media darlings as the "McLibel Two."

Steel and Morris kept McDonald's tied up in court for seven years—the longest-running trial in English history. Technically speaking, McDonald's won the case, since the judge ultimately ordered Steel and Morris to pay £40,000. That judgment, however, came after McDonald's had spent an estimated £10 million on legal fees—a fact that helps to illustrate why tort law is such a hit with the legal profession. And tort is not even the sexiest topic in the law. Sex is. Turn the page for details.

5

SEX AND THE CITIZEN

Kerb-crawling: importuning [a prostitute] from a motor vehicle. See Sexual Offences Act 1985.

— L. B. CURZON, *DICTIONARY OF LAW*

A 95-year-old man has been arrested during a crackdown on kerb-crawlers at a popular seaside resort.

— *EVENING STANDARD,* SEPTEMBER 21, 2006

Until January 2005, unmarried persons could not have sex in Virginia. At least, not legally.

Those who attempted the feat—and anecdotal evidence suggests that there were more than a few—were guilty of the crime of **fornication**. Indeed, fornication would probably still be a crime in the Old Dominion were it not for a determined woman named Muguet Martin.

It all began in 2001, when Muguet started dating Kristopher Ziherl. For nearly two years, everything seemed to go swimmingly. Muguet and Kristopher enjoyed all of the hand-holding, giggling, and occasional canoodling that comes with young love. But trouble arrived in paradise when Muguet discovered that Kristopher had bestowed upon her a case of genital herpes. She broke up with Kristopher and promptly sued him for all he was worth.

Kristopher—the cad—fought the lawsuit. He argued that Muguet had no right to compensation since she had contracted herpes while committing fornication. The trial judge agreed with Kristopher and dismissed the lawsuit. Undaunted, Muguet appealed all the way up to the Virginia Supreme Court which, on January 14, 2005, struck down the antifornication law, allowing Muguet's suit to go forward.

And now Virginia is for lovers! Well, actually, it's only for lovers who stay behind closed doors. The Virginia Supreme Court took pains to point out that the Commonwealth can still arrest people for **public fornication**.

Fornication was originally an architectural term, deriving from the Latin *fornix,* an arched or vaulted chamber. In Roman times, prostitutes used to gather under archways;

thus *fornix* became a code word for brothel. The word ultimately stems from *fornax,* which means oven. Roman ovens
had vaulted domes, like those you find in your neighborhood brick-oven pizza joint. Strange as it may seem, then,
"fornication" and "furnace" come from the same root. Or
perhaps not so strange when one considers that up to the
seventeenth century, "hothouse" was a common slang term
for brothel. In any event, fornication, variously spelled *forni-
cacion* and *fornycacyoun,* has been recorded in English since
the fourteenth century.

Fornication laws prohibit consensual sex involving
unmarried persons, and such laws are very old. The Virginia law that Muguet and Kristopher violated, for example, was enacted when Thomas Jefferson was in the
White House. Before that, colonial Virginia had laws punishing fornication with female servants at least as early as
1658. If the fornication led to pregnancy, the father might
have to the pay the servant's master as much as fifteen hundred pounds of tobacco. By an interesting coincidence,
tobacco production in Virginia skyrocketed during this
period.

Virginia was not the only state to hold on to its fornication law well into the twentieth century. Ten other states
still have such laws on their books. As recently as 2003,
the State of Georgia prosecuted a fornication case. In
1996, officials in Gem County, Idaho, announced a campaign to enforce that state's fornication laws.

A WOMAN SCORNED

Perhaps the best thing about the language of sex laws is how
well it illustrates that the laws themselves are completely,

almost charmingly, disconnected from the facts of modern life.

Take marital infidelity. While sophisticated types like to brush it off ("it meant nothing"), the law retains a Dickensian lexicon to describe the dire consequences of this all-too-common indiscretion. If a married person sleeps with an unmarried person, for example, only the former commits the crime of **adultery**, while the latter commits fornication and possibly **solicitation of chastity**, which is the crime of asking another person to commit adultery or fornication. The wronged spouse, meanwhile, not only has the right to sue the cheating spouse for **divorce**, but can also sue the interloper under the torts of **criminal conversation** and **alienation of affection**. Each of these legal concepts still has some claim to validity in one part of America or another.

Seven states allow a jilted spouse to sue a person who has intercourse with the other spouse for criminal conversation, typically shortened to **crim. con.** "Conversation" here refers to sexual intercourse, a usage once favored by Shakespeare but now obsolete everywhere but in legalese. Most people who sue for crim. con. also sue for **alienation of affection**, which requires the plaintiff to prove that there was "genuine affection" between the spouses before an intruder spoiled things. At least the plaintiff doesn't have to prove that there was a full-fledged *conversation*—even some light banter will do.

Criminal conversation lawsuits were abolished in England in 1857, but they continue to play surprisingly well on the other side of the Atlantic. In 2001, a North Carolina jury awarded $2 million to the plaintiff in such a case, breaking the previous record of $1.2 million set in 1997. In North Carolina alone, over two hundred alienation and crim. con. cases arc filed every year.

More than twenty states treat adultery as a crime. And these are not obsolete laws of the "you may not chew tobacco on a Sunday" variety. In recent decades, adultery cases have been tried in states as diverse as Alabama, Massachusetts, and Pennsylvania. So when television legal analyst Greta Van Susteren declared in 1998 that "an extramarital affair . . . is not illegal," she wasn't so much analyzing the law as making it up.

In 2004, an adultery prosecution in Virginia (Is it something in the water?) made headlines around the country. The defendant, John Bushey, was a married small-town lawyer in his sixties who had taken up with a shapely divorcée named Nellie Mae Hensley. After the affair had run its course, Bushey returned to his wife of eighteen years, while Hensley—evidently unconcerned about her own reputation—told police about the fling. As a single woman, Hensley was in the clear, but Bushey was charged with criminal adultery.

Bushey vowed to fight the charges. The ACLU rushed to his aid, apparently eager to strike down what it viewed as an outmoded law. At the same time, a considerable number of self-proclaimed "values voters" came out in support of Virginia's right to prosecute. This had all the makings of a landmark case, but Bushey grew tired of litigation even faster than he had grown tired of Nellie Mae. He threw in the towel and accepted twenty hours of community service as punishment for his crime.

Committing adultery has nothing to do—linguistically speaking—with being an adult. "Adult" comes from the Latin *adultus,* which is the past participle of *adolescere* (to grow up). Adultery, which over the ages has been known as *avowtery, advoutrie, aduoutrie, aduoultrie, adoultry,* and *adultry* before settling into its present spelling, stems from *adulterare,* also Latin but meaning to corrupt or spoil. Straying from one's spouse literally "adulterates" a marriage.

There are plenty of synonyms for adultery, but few of them have ever gained legal currency. The Anglo-Saxons called it **aewbryce,** which literally means "marriage breaking" but, significantly, was also used to describe lawbreaking in general. The word survived well after the Norman Conquest, making its last appearance as *eaubruche* in 1225.

President Clinton was widely mocked for stating that he and Monica Lewinsky did not have "sexual relations"—meaning intercourse—just a blow job, thank you. Nonetheless, the distinction drawn by Clinton does matter where adultery is concerned. Many states, including the District of Columbia, still rely on the common law definition of adultery, in which sexual intercourse is a necessary element. In 2003, the Supreme Court of New Hampshire held that a wife who engaged in a lesbian affair did not commit adultery, since intercourse could not have taken place. In Maryland, just over the border from D.C., at least one judge has held that *any* sexual act might constitute adultery. Just as well for Bill, then, that he didn't take Monica up to Bethesda for the evening.

What is now known as date rape was traditionally known to the law as **seduction**, a tort (see Chapter 4) or sometimes a crime (see Chapter 6) committed by a man who induces an unmarried woman of good reputation to have sexual intercourse. The rationale behind this law was to compensate fathers for the loss of services of working daughters who were impregnated by unscrupulous men. It apparently did not matter if the man sent flowers and chocolates the next day. This ancient tort still clings to life in a number of states, including North Carolina where it became the subject of a 2003 lawsuit. In that case, a female student at Duke University sued a campus fraternity, and one of its pledges, for "wrongful seduction."

Unlike date rape, **incest**, from the Latin *incestum* (unchaste), is illegal whether or not there was genuine consent. The scope of the term, however, differs from place to place. Most countries do not share the American tendency to forbid first-cousin marriage, let alone fornication. In Britain, there appears to be a certain confusion surrounding the meaning of incest. There, a man arrested for having sex with his twenty-two-year-old daughter pleaded for leniency on the basis that the daughter was "more like a sister to me."

A SCOOP OF RUM BUGGERY

There is something comical about the sound of "buggery." The schoolboy naughtiness of the word goes back at least as far as Winston Churchill's remark that the only traditions of the Royal Navy are "rum, buggery, and the lash"—making anal sex sound vaguely like a flavor of ice cream.

And despite its perceived silliness, buggery actually is a technical legal term in England and in a number of American states. The word is a corruption of "Bulgar," as in a person from Bulgaria. In the Middle Ages, Bulgaria was a center of Manichaeism, a religious heresy whose members were accused of committing unnatural sex acts. To call somebody a Bulgar became a wink-wink, nudge-nudge way to accuse a man of homosexuality.

In most American states, as well as in Scotland, the legal equivalent of buggery is **sodomy**. Although the term clearly derives from the biblical story of Sodom and Gomorrah, the logic behind that derivation is somewhat skewed. It is true that both Sodom and Gomorrah were said to be wicked, but the Bible does not actually specify that *sexual* wickedness was the problem. Nor does the Bible refer to "sodomites" except to describe people who lived in Sodom, which would include Lot and his family. The big loser in all of this is Gomorrah, whose name does not lend itself well to adjectival forms. Not that people haven't tried. Attempts were made in the sixteenth century to refer to practices that were *Gomorrhean* or even *Gomorreal:* words too ugly even for lawyers.

Buggery was the first sexual activity to attract the attention of secular law. Before the sixteenth century, that sort of thing was the exclusive province of church authorities. When England broke away from the Catholic Church, Henry VIII took it upon himself to legislate sexual morality—this from a man who married six times and beheaded two of his wives. At Henry's bidding, in 1533 Parliament outlawed buggery, defining it only as "a detestable and abominable vice" which could be committed "with mankind or beast." They could almost be referring to jogging.

In the late eighteenth century, Blackstone, who typically spared no detail in describing virtually every law in effect in Britain, became curiously terse on the subject of buggery. In his *Commentaries,* he defined it simply as "**a crime against nature**," leaving concerned citizens to wonder whether it might apply to, say, chopping down trees.

THE BRITISH ARE COMING

Although Henry VIII's statute was ambiguous at best, the English courts quickly arrived at a definition of buggery: It meant anal intercourse. And buggery was buggery whether it occurred between two men or between a man and a woman. As a matter of law, **intercourse** (natural or unnatural) refers to a sexual connection involving **penetration**. By the eighteenth century, British courts required an additional element for buggery: what the judges euphemistically called **emission**. It is no doubt a source of pride for the English judiciary that, centuries before global warming, they had enacted the world's first emissions controls.

That's as far as buggery got in the U.K. All forms of sexual conduct other than anal intercourse remained technically lawful in Britain until Victorian legislation criminalized **gross indecency** between males. Gross indecency was never precisely defined, but whatever it was, Oscar Wilde was found guilty of it in 1895. The charges had been pressed by John Douglas, the Marquess of Queensberry, who was furious over Wilde's dalliance with his son, Lord Alfred Douglas. The case might not have been brought at all had Wilde not first attempted to sue Queensberry for libel (see Chapter 4) for denouncing him as a "somdomite"—spelling was not Queensberry's forte.

Wilde's failed libel suit led directly to a criminal trial in which prosecutors summoned a parade of young men to testify in vivid detail about their roles in Wilde's sexual antics. After one jury was deadlocked, a second jury convicted the playwright. Wilde was sentenced to spend two years packed in with hundreds of hardened criminals at Reading Gaol (*please, don't throw me in the briar patch!*).

In America, sodomy and buggery remained felonies (the most serious category of crime) in many states until the United States Supreme Court struck down antisodomy laws in the 2003 case of *Lawrence* v. *Texas*. At the time of that decision, fourteen states and Puerto Rico still had enforceable sodomy laws. Even after *Lawrence,* certain aspects of state sodomy laws remain legally valid. According to the Louisiana Supreme Court, for example, laws characterizing oral sex as "a crime against nature" are still partially valid. In 2005, that court upheld a felony sodomy charge, with a possible sentence of five years, against a woman who offered to perform oral sex for money. Had she offered the more "natural" intercourse instead of oral sex, the penalty would have been far less severe.

American politicians, by and large, displayed little creativity when it came to writing sodomy laws. They shamelessly lifted the language of Henry VIII and Blackstone, combining **abominable**, **detestable**, and **crime against nature** in as many permutations as mathematically possible. Lest one get bollixed up by buggery language, the following table may help to guide one through the pre-*Lawrence* sodomy laws:

IN . . .	WHOEVER COMMITS . . .	IS GUILTY OF . . .
Arizona, California, and Idaho	the infamous crime against nature	sodomy or crime against nature
Indiana, Massachusetts, Michigan, and Rhode Island	the abominable and detestable crime against nature	sodomy or buggery
Mississippi and Oklahoma	the detestable and abominable crime against nature	unnatural intercourse or crime against nature
South Carolina	the abominable crime of buggery	buggery

Although the American states slavishly copied British terms, they did not always give them British definitions. In some instances, courts and legislatures were not willing to attach *any* meaning to sodomy or related terms. The reasons for their reticence were not very convincing, or consistent. One New Jersey court explained that judges avoided describing sodomy out of a "great concern for delicacy." A California court refused to define "crime against nature" on the basis that its meaning was "obvious," while an Ohio court claimed it was "impossible to define." In two cases from the 1950s, the New Hampshire Supreme Court attempted to explain the scope of that state's sodomy laws without giving a single specific example of behavior that might be prohibited. The Supreme Court did not utter the word "homosexual" until 1952.

Some American lawyers refuse even to use the word "sodomy," let alone define it, instead referring elliptically to "the crime not fit to be named," another phrase coined by Blackstone. These words were translated by some lawyer into the more esoteric-sounding *crimen innominatum,* which is nothing more than Latin for "the nameless crime." Now *that's* three years of law school well spent.

In one sodomy prosecution from 1921, a Florida judge furiously rejected the idea of discussing the crime at issue with this tirade:

> A discussion of the loathsome, revolting crime would be of no edification to the people, nor interest to the members of the bar.

The gentleman doth protest too much, methinks.

When American courts did attempt to define sodomy, they often disagreed with their British counterparts. In the 1905 case of *People* v. *Carroll,* a California court took the unusual position—contrary to English precedents—that sodomy could take place only between men. In that case, a man named John Carroll had been tried and convicted of committing the "crime against nature" with one Frank Derby. The appellate court reversed the conviction because the original complaint had failed to allege that Frank Derby was a man. The fact that the police alleged a "crime against nature" did not prove anything, said the court, because the legal term for homosexual sex was "the *infamous* crime against nature." Without the word "infamous" and without specifically saying that Derby was a man, the prosecution had not presented their case properly. Frankie and Johnny may have been lovers, but that's as far as the court would go.

An almost identical case arose in California just nine

THE
PARTY
OF THE
FIRST
PART

100

years later. In *People* v. *Allison* (1914), an appeals court overturned the conviction of James Allison, who had been prosecuted for engaging in sodomy with Frank B. Love. Once again, the prosecutors—will they never learn?—failed to allege in the indictment that Frank was a man. They did remember to include the word "infamous" before "crime against nature," but the only specific description of the crime was that Allison had had "carnal knowledge" of Frank Love. As a matter of law, the court held that the term **carnal knowledge** refers strictly to heterosexual sex, and therefore Frank must have been Francine. There was no crime against nature.

In the 1812 case of *Commonwealth* v. *Thomas,* Virginia became the first state to reject the British requirement that emission is a necessary part of sodomy. Evidence of penetration alone would suffice to convict a man of the crime against nature. Most states eventually followed Virginia's lead, while others stuck to the British rule of "If he did not emit, you must acquit."

The most important difference between the United States and the Mother Country was that American states generally did not create a separate offense of gross indecency. Instead, courts and legislatures expanded the definition of sodomy to cover all forms of **deviate sexual conduct**, which is a catchall legal term referring to any consensual activity other than vaginal intercourse that might be even slightly gratifying. As a result, the legal meaning of sodomy has always been a moving target.

Lesbian sex is sometimes included in sodomy and sometimes not. Under the common law, crimes against nature did not include lesbianism. This was for the curious reason, as one nineteenth-century British court held, that sex between women "has no existence." Presumably, this meant that the act of sex required the presence of at least one penis in the room. Or perhaps the notion that women were off having sex together was simply too much for the law to concede. In 1971, when the State of Oklahoma brought sodomy charges against a lesbian, the defendant argued that "it would be legally impossible for two women to commit the crime against nature." The judges disagreed, but only after they had—as they rather boastfully announced—conducted an "exhaustive search" of the literature on lesbians and the law.

Does sodomy include oral sex? Experts disagree. A 1973 study showed that twelve states said no, sixteen states said yes, and others had more subtle answers, depending on whether the participants were male or female—and in what combination. As a legal matter, it often comes down to the definition of **penetration** or **sexual penetration**. English law held that where sodomy was concerned, penetration meant anal sex, not oral sex. In 1913, the Supreme Court of Oregon became one of the first to take a contrary position, deciding, as a later commentator romantically put it, "it is as much against nature to make sexual entry at one end of the alimentary canal as at the other."

Other states remained steadfastly traditional. In the 1953 Morrison case, the New Jersey court ruled that oral sex did not constitute the sort of penetration required for sodomy. In the course of his lengthy opinion on the matter, the judge did concede that the diverse sodomy cases from other states "contain much that is instructive and thought-provoking." What sort of thoughts, one can't help but wonder, did those cases provoke?

In 1915, **fellatio** and **cunnilingus** officially entered the

THE
PARTY
OF THE
FIRST
PART

102

legal vocabulary. In that year, the California legislature became the first to use those words in a statute (for the express purpose of outlawing both). Four years later, the California Supreme Court struck down the law, saying that "fellatio" and "cunnilingus" are not words in "ordinary use" in English, as the California constitution required for all statutes. Faced with the challenge of describing fellatio and cunnilingus in "ordinary" English, the legislature passed a law banning **oral copulation**, leaving many Californians yearning for the day when they could just have oral sex.

Other states used even more obscure language. Oregon's sodomy law prohibited "**osculatory relations** with the private parts of any man, woman, or child." *Osculatory* is mainly a term of mathematics and geometry, signifying curves; but it can also refer to kissing. And who among us has not been tempted, in the heat of the moment, to cry out, "Osculate me, you fool!"?

In 1938, a Georgia court had to answer the seemingly novel question of whether sodomy included **interfemoral** (that is, between-the-thighs) stimulation; in fact, the issue had already been considered by British courts. The British had said yes; Georgia, no. Incidentally, in some places, urinating on another person can constitute sodomy. Heaven knows, it's bad manners no matter what you call it.

I LOVE EWE

The statute of Henry VIII states that buggery can take place "with mankind or beast." Ever since then, the legal definition of buggery and sodomy has included **bestiality**, that is, sex between a human being and an animal. Even this relatively simple proposition, however, begets some shades of meaning. While most states include bestiality within a single sodomy law, Kentucky and New Jersey decided—with no etymological justification—to make "sodomy" the legal term for "unnatural" sex between humans, and "buggery" the legal term for bestiality. Typically, the law prohibits the "crime against nature" with any animal, but Virginia outlaws sex only with a **brute animal**. This language raises at least the possibility that sex with a domesticated animal is legal in Virginia, but to date there has not been a test case for that proposition.

THE
PARTY
OF THE
FIRST
PART

104

Bestiality cases continue to arise on both sides of the Atlantic. In 2002, an Englishman named Stephen Hall was sent to prison for six months for "buggery with an animal committed in the open air." The victim was a goat. In the United States, the Supreme Court's decision in *Lawrence* v. *Texas* allows states to continue to enforce laws against those who love animals a little overmuch. An Iowa man was prosecuted for this particular crime against nature in 2002, having been caught in a hayloft in postcoital *tristesse* after violating a sheep. In many places such acts now come under laws against **cruelty to animals**, but as recently as 2006, a Michigan man was charged with sodomy after having sex with a sheep. He was sent to prison for up to twenty years, and his name was permanently added to Michigan's register of sex offenders.

Sodomy is one area of the law where plain language would have saved everyone a lot of trouble. And yet, in those comparatively rare instances when lawmakers did spell out sodomy in graphic detail, one almost wishes they hadn't. The fact that Connecticut saw fit to include sexual conduct with a "dead body" under the sodomy umbrella tells us more, perhaps, than we wanted to know about the Nutmeg State. And then there is the alarming specificity of North Dakota's sodomy ban, which extends to carnal knowledge of "any animal *or bird.*"

In Texas, **deviate sexual intercourse** is defined with a precision worthy of those insert-tab-A-into-slot-B furniture assembly manuals: "any contact between any part of the genitals of one person and the mouth or anus of another person; or the penetration of the genitals or the anus of another person with an object."

SELF-HELP

All sodomy laws have at least one common theme: The perpetrator must have a partner, human or animal. It took the law some time to deal with the perennial problem of sex with inanimate objects.

In 1876, Ohio became the first state to prohibit **instruments** used for "self-pollution," and they were not referring to cigarettes. In 1894 the law was broadened to include any "instrument or other article of an indecent or immoral nature." These were the first American laws against **sex toys**.

Sex toys continue to interest state legislators. In 1998, Alabama passed a law prohibiting the sale of "any device designed or marketed as useful primarily for the stimulation of human genital organs." The good news is that it's still easy to buy guns in Birmingham.

Soon after the law was passed, Sherri Williams, the owner of two adult novelty shops, challenged it in court.

A federal district court agreed with Williams, finding that the law violated Alabamans' constitutional "right to use sexual devices like . . . vibrators, dildos, anal beads, and artificial vaginas."

If you're tempted to pull out your Pocket Constitution in search of references to anal beads, I'm afraid you're in for a disappointment. The district court was referring to a **penumbral right** (from the Latin *penumbra* or "partial shadow"); that is, a right that is not actually mentioned in the Constitution but that can be inferred from other rights. This concept derives from the Supreme Court's 1965 decision in *Griswold* v. *Connecticut*, in which the Court held that the right to use contraceptives exists in the penumbra of the Bill of Rights.

Turning back to Alabama, in 2004 a federal appellate court overturned the district court's decision, holding that there is no constitutional right, not even a penumbral right, to use sex toys. That decision was written by Judge Stanley F. Birch, who emphasized that the Alabama law defines "sex toy" very narrowly. According to the judge, the law would not prohibit the sale of such things as "ordinary vibrators," provided they were not designed "primarily for the stimulation of genital organs"—leaving the door wide open for the sale of vibrators designed primarily for making cappuccino.

Judge Birch even reassured Alabamans that they could buy sex toys out of state and bring them home. At the very least, these fine distinctions should make for some interesting law enforcement banter:

> "Mr. Ziherl, do you know how fast you were going?"
>
> "Well, officer—"

THE
PARTY
OF THE
FIRST
PART

106

"Hold the phone! Is that an artificial vagina on the seat next to you?"

"Yes, officer, but I bought it in Virginia. That's where I used to live until—well, it's a long story."

"How do I know where you bought it? You got a receipt for that thing?"

"No, sir."

"Then you're going to have to tell me: What is the *primary* use of that there artificial vagina?"

Six other states outlaw the sale of sex toys. In 2004, a Texas woman was charged under the sex toy law, for organizing "passion parties," which are latter-day Tupperware parties used to promote the sale of various sexual devices. Oddly enough, had she sold the devices as **novelty items**— *Now here's an interesting paperweight!*—it would have been perfectly legal.

Although sex toys may be contraband, no state has ever attempted to prohibit private, non-mechanically-aided acts of **masturbation**—a word thought to derive from Latin *manus* (hand) plus *stuprare* (to defile). **Public** acts of masturbation, however, can be prosecuted—making it highly relevant to know how the law defines "public." For many years, any act taking place within a closed toilet stall was considered sufficiently public for the purpose of these laws. Vice squads routinely peeked into toilet stalls looking for any sort of group or individual sexual activity. Such tactics are no longer lawful now that the courts have held that people have a reasonable expectation of privacy within a toilet stall. The last conviction for solitary masturbation in a toilet stall took place in

Idaho in 1990. The name of the man arrested was—wait for it—*Limberhand.*

IT'S A BUSINESS DOING PLEASURE WITH YOU

When sex is performed, or even offered, in exchange for money, we have a case of **prostitution**.

Prostitute comes from a Latin word (*prostituere*) meaning "to stand before," which gradually acquired the meaning of "to offer publicly." It entered the English language late in the sixteenth century amid stiff competition, since the British were already on speaking terms with the Anglo-Saxon whore, the French *harlot,* and the strumpet of unknown origin. Nonetheless, "prostitute" became the favored legal term, perhaps because it was more modern and clinical-sounding.

Legal lexicographers, seemingly confused about the supply-and-demand dynamics of the skin trade, traditionally defined prostitution as a function of *women's* debauchery. One representative law dictionary from the early twentieth century defines prostitute as "a female given to indiscriminate lewdness," and prostitution as "the common lewdness of a woman for gain." A popular movement in the late 1800s applied the label "prostitute" to any married woman who had sex with her husband for any reason other than procreation. *Not tonight, dear, it would be a felony.*

In a similar vein, Blackstone explains that a wife may be indicted and set in a **pillory** (a wooden frame used for punishment) with her husband for keeping a brothel, "for this is an offence . . . in which the wife has the principal share, and is such an offence as the law presumes to be

THE
PARTY
OF THE
FIRST
PART

108

generally conducted by the intrigue of the female sex." A nineteenth-century print depicting prostitutes in Manhattan offering themselves to respectable-looking men is entitled "Hooking the Victim." This metaphor would appear to be the origin of the term **hooker**, an American usage first recorded in 1845.

The moralizing impulses of the Victorian era put an end to the policy of benign neglect in which prostitution, while not exactly legal, was tolerated. Indeed, sometimes it was even regulated. During the Middle Ages, the City of London enacted what may have been the first **consumer protection law** for the benefit of **johns**; it provided that "no single woman [shall] take mony to lye with any man, except she lye with him all night, till the morrow."

In 2004, the Liverpool City Council voted in favor of a plan to create official red-light districts, although Liverpool calls them **managed prostitution zones**. The Liverpool plan was reportedly the result of an extensive "sex worker consultation" led by Mark Bellis, a local university professor (*Why, Professor, is that an ivory tower or are you just happy to see me?*). Predictably, some area residents have threatened legal action if the prostitution zone ends up too close to their homes.

The modern sex industry has its own trade organizations, most notably COYOTE, which stands for Call Off Your Old Tired Ethics, founded by Margo St. James in 1973. St. James and others insist that engaging in prostitution is actually a feminist right. They have pressed for the replacement of "prostitute" with the more politically correct **sex worker**. So far, the term has been picked up, so to speak, by a number of law school journals, but the law has yet to adopt it.

Like all true professionals, a prostitute needs an agent, sometimes known as a **ponce** (possibly from *pounce*) or a **procurer**. In American law, such a person is usually referred to as a **panderer** or sometimes just plain **pander**; the activity is **pandering**. These terms come from the mythological figure Pandarus, a Trojan archer who is said to have procured for Troilus the love of Cressida. Pander, or pandar, was used to denote a sexual go-between as early as 1450, but Shakespeare greatly reinforced the usage in his play *Troilus and Cressida* (1609), when he has Pandarus say, "Let all pittifull goers betweene be cald to the worlds end after my name, call them all Panders."

Pimp is another word for pander, more of a slang term perhaps, but still recognized in legal dictionaries. "Pimp" was first used in English around 1600, but where it came from is decidedly unclear. The *Oxford English Dictionary* speculates that pimp might be related to the Old French *pimpant,* meaning alluring or seductive in appearance, but concedes that this suggestion "leaves much to be explained." Be that as it may, the word certainly caught on after 1600. English law even recognized a form of landholding known as **Pimp Tenure**, by which the right to occupy land depended on the keeping of a certain number of whores for the King or the King's army.

Yet another term for this profession—and it's always interesting to see where a language lavishes its attention—is **bawd**, from which we get the adjective **bawdy**. This word dates from the fourteenth century and is probably an abbreviation of an even older French word *bawdstrot,* meaning "procurer of prostitutes."

Bawd also gives rise to **bawdy house**, an early term for **brothel**. The latter is technically suspect, though, since a brothel is really an Old English word for "a ruined or degenerate person." The term *brothel's house* was shortened to "brothel," and then got mixed up with the similar-sounding term *bordel,* related to the Italian *bordello.* The law recognizes both "bawdy house" and "brothel," as well as the sternly Victorian **house of ill fame**.

You would think that in Nevada, where prostitution is legal in most counties, the statutes might dump the old pejorative terms for sex establishments and come up with something more neutral—like "sex establishment," come to think of it. Instead, Nevada law speaks with the same puritanical zeal as the other states. In Storey County, for example, a sex establishment is officially called a house of ill fame; in Nye County, it's a brothel; in Lyons County, it can be either of those, as well as a bawdy house.

Outside Nevada, prostitution may result in a number of distinct crimes. In most places, the prostitute commits a crime by selling sex, but so does the client—the crime of **solicitation**. The pimp commits the crime of pandering. Federal law makes it illegal to transport a woman across state lines "for the purpose of prostitution, or debauchery, or any other immoral purpose." This law is known as the **Mann Act**; its full name is the "Mann White Slave Traffic Act." **White slavery** is a nineteenth-century term referring to girls—and often with the specific sense of virgins—forced into prostitution. Embarrassingly enough, the phrase (presumably meant to distinguish the girls from that *other* type of slave) remained an official statutory term in the United States until 1986.

Cigarette, anyone?

6

ARRESTING LANGUAGE

Wobbler: n. *California Law. An offense that is punishable either as a felony or as a misdemeanor.*

— RANDOM HOUSE WEBSTER'S
DICTIONARY OF THE LAW

On the evening of July 23, 1971, a young Englishman named Stephen Collins went down to the local pub and had a few pints. A few too many, in fact. He stumbled home to find that one of his neighbors—an eighteen-year-old woman for whom he had long lusted—was sleeping with her window wide open. Collins positioned a stepladder near the open window, climbed up, and took a peek. What he saw was the object of his affections sleeping in the nude.

Collins rushed down the ladder and took off all his clothes—except, for some reason, his socks. He went back up the ladder and perched on the windowsill. The young woman awoke to see the outlines of a naked young man who was, as it were, standing very much at attention. Still drowsy, the woman assumed the randy visitor to be her boyfriend and, to Collins's astonishment, beckoned him into her bed.

It was only after some hurried intercourse that the young woman realized something was amiss. She turned on her bedside lamp, slapped Collins in the face, bit him on the arm, and ran to the bathroom.

Collins was arrested and charged with **burglary**, which, although often thought of as a species of theft, refers to an unlawful entry into a building—also known as **breaking and entering**—with the intent to commit any serious crime. The crime that a burglar intends to commit often *is* theft, but it need not be. In this case, prosecutors charged that Collins had entered the house intent on raping his nubile neighbor. He was not charged with rape, presumably because the victim had consented to intercourse, albeit due to a case of mistaken identity.

After he was convicted by a jury, Collins took his case to the Court of Appeals. He argued that his entry into the house had been perfectly lawful; after all, the young lady had invited him in. Nonsense, said the prosecution, Collins had already "entered" the house when the woman gestured to him.

It all came down to this: What exactly is the "entering" in breaking and entering? Had Collins entered the house while teetering on the windowsill? Was he on the outside portion of the sill or the inside portion of the sill? These were the critical questions, but they were never presented to the jury. The Court of Appeals had no choice but to overturn Collins's conviction. And with that, Stephen Collins—having bedded the woman of his dreams and then been set free on a technicality—disappears from the pages of legal history, no doubt scarcely able to believe his luck.

One final distinguishing feature of *Collins:* it contains the most famous judicial discussion of socks in the English language. When reciting the Court of Appeals decision, Lord Justice Davies took a detour to consider the interesting, but legally irrelevant, fact that Collins had kept his socks on when he ventured up the ladder. This curious behavior troubled the Lord Justice. Why had Collins done it?

"Apparently," said Davies, "[Collins] took the view that if the girl's mother entered the bedroom it would be easier to effect a rapid escape if he had his socks on than if he was in his bare feet. That is a matter about which we are not called upon to express any view, and would in any event find ourselves unable to express one."

Sartorial questions aside, the Collins case perfectly illustrates the ways in which guilt and innocence often hinge on very narrow interpretations of legal language. The question of Collins's "entry" into the young lady's house was "as narrow," said Lord Justice Davies, "as the window sill which is crucial to this case." As we shall see, semantic battles are often fought in the criminal courts. So often, in fact, it will knock your socks off.

CRIMINAL SENTENCES

THE
PARTY
OF THE
FIRST
PART

116

Verbal mistakes carry a high price in criminal law. It is the only branch of the law that allows the State to deprive a citizen of his liberty or even, depending on where one lives, his life. From another perspective, criminal law is the only thing standing between us and the bad guys. Either way you look at it, criminal law ought to be written in language so clear that the general public, and those who serve on juries, can readily understand it.

How hard can that be? Few topics have greater immediacy and drama than crime. It livens up the evening news and the morning papers. Dozens of television shows follow the daily routine of cops and prosecutors. Millions of people devote entire beach holidays to reading about crime and punishment in all their exquisite gore.

But once you put all this fascinating stuff through the legal machinery, you end up with garden variety legalese, liberally sprinkled with archaic terms, vague standards, technical jargon, and Latin. Criminal codes suffer from an ancient prejudice: the idea that each individual law, with all its conditions and exceptions, must be packed into a single sentence.

The logic behind this practice is that a sentence is a "self-contained unit," and therefore one cannot with any confidence modify one sentence with another sentence. As a matter of English composition, the notion expressed in the preceding sentence is absurd, as this sentence demonstrates.

Nonetheless, criminal statutes continue to suffer under the legacy of the sentences-on-steroids philosophy. One California penal statute consists of a single sentence of 150 words (by way of comparison, the mean sentence length in scientific writing is 28 words). A section of the British Road Traffic Act of 1972, which defines various moving violations, consists of a 740-word sentence. The whole problem with criminal law, one might say, is that the sentences are too long.

Not to be melodramatic, but this *is* a matter of life and death. As we saw in Chapter 3, juries in capital cases often find themselves struggling to understand terms like **aggravating**, **mitigating**, and the ever-slippery **reasonable doubt**. Criminal cases have been won or lost on the basis of fine points of syntax and punctuation.

Consider the expression **and/or**. Invented by commercial lawyers to indicate situations in which various combinations of options are acceptable—"shipments may be received in Newark and/or Brooklyn"—it has been carelessly dropped into dozens of criminal cases like so many mischievous stink bombs. Suppose a person is convicted of violating law A and/or law B: Should he suffer the penalty for A or B or both? If law B is later found to be unconstitutional, should the conviction be overturned, or can we safely assume that law A was also violated?

In 1936, the Texas Court of Criminal Appeals tossed out a conviction for gambling because the indictment charged the defendant with wagering on "cards, dice and/or dominoes," leaving the record unclear as to exactly which game(s) the defendant had been playing. In 1941, a New Jersey Court dismissed a complaint for disorderly conduct because it contained the expression "and/or" which has been "emphatically condemned." In 1947, the New Mexico Supreme Court referred to and/or as a "linguistic abomination" and in 1954, a North Carolina judge called it a "monstrous linguistic abomination." Seven years later, a United States military court blasted the expression as "the abominable combination of conjunctive and disjunctive." Apart from sodomy (see Chapter 5), it would be difficult to find any practice that has inspired more judges to use the word **abomination**.

In at least two cases, men's lives have been left dangling from the merest comma. The first was *U.S.* v. *Palmer* (1818), in which the Supreme Court considered the fate of three New Englanders—John Palmer, Thomas Wilson, and Barney Colloghan—who had stolen $92,000 (about $1.4 million in current dollars) worth of cargo from a Spanish ship, including rum, sugar, gold, and "ten hogsheads of coffee."

The trial court had hopelessly deadlocked on the question of whether the three men had violated the federal piracy statute, which mandated the death penalty for any person who:

> shall commit upon the high seas . . . murder or
> robbery, or any other offence, which, if committed

THE
PARTY
OF THE
FIRST
PART

118

within the body of a county, would by the laws of the United States, be punishable with death.

The key to the case was determining exactly what was modified by the clause "which, if committed within the body of a county, would . . . be punishable with death." If the clause modified everything beginning with "murder or robbery," then the men were safe, because, although they had committed robbery on the high seas, it was not the sort of robbery that would have been punishable with death had it occurred on American soil.

The majority of the court, however, decided that the clause modified only the immediately preceding words, "any other offence." On that reading, *any* robbery committed on the high seas would constitute piracy. The court was evidently influenced by the fact that the words "or any other offence" was set off by commas. This reasoning led Justice Johnson to write a stinging dissent in which he declared, "These men's lives may depend upon a comma. . . . [I]f ever forced to choose between obeying the court on such a point, or resigning my commission, I would not hesitate adopting the latter alternative." In the end, Johnson did not have to resign from the court, since the justices were able to agree that the United States lacked jurisdiction over the particular case. Palmer, Wilson, and Colloghan went free, even though the forces of punctuation were against them.

One hundred years later, an Englishman named Roger Casement was not so lucky. In 1917, Casement was convicted by a British court under the Treason Act of 1351 for lending a helping hand to the Kaiser in World War I. Casement argued that the lower court had misinterpreted the Treason Act because modern publishers had carelessly inserted commas where they did not belong.

One of the judges, the splendidly named Justice Darling, was sufficiently intrigued by Casement's argument to stroll over to the Public Record Office, magnifying glass in hand, and examine the original fourteenth-century statute. The scrupulous judge found several forward slashes, known in Latin as *virgules*—these were the immediate predecessor of the comma—just where they were supposed to be. Casement was hanged as a traitor.

How does one avoid a fate such as that which befell Roger Casement? First, don't commit treason. Second, get to know the language of criminal law, virgules and all.

MEN BEHAVING BADLY

Looking over the names of some of today's more stimulating crimes, we find such familiar terms as:

Murder
Manslaughter
Mayhem
Battery
Assault
Theft

These words generally derive from an earthy mixture of Anglo-Saxon and Anglo-Norman. All of them have been around for at least five hundred years, some for a thousand years or more. And yet, they sound perfectly modern to our ears—indeed, they leap off the pages of the tabloids every morning.

They are all **felonies**, which comes from an Old French word (*felonie*) meaning wickedness. The word illustrates the influence of the medieval church on the law; crime was not merely disorderly, but a form of wickedness requiring punishment or atonement. Punishment was serious business—a convicted felon would have to forfeit all of his lands and goods to the Crown. On the bright side, the felon scarcely had a chance to miss his things, since he also forfeited his life.

Felonies are sometimes referred to as **capital crimes** because they required **capital punishment** ("capital" coming from the Latin *caput,* or head). Executions themselves had a highly ritualized legal language. Well into the nineteenth century, American judges would sentence a convicted felon to be "hung by the neck until you are dead, dead, dead," which would seem to be rubbing it in a bit. According to legal folklore, the repetition of "dead" was required to justify two additional attempts to hang a man if the executioner failed on the first try.

Less serious crimes are known as **misdemeanors** from the Middle English *mysdemeanour*—literally, bad demeanor or bad conduct. A misdemeanor conviction might get you a fine or a stint in prison. The distinction between felonies and misdemeanors is now somewhat hazy, since felonies no longer necessarily entail beheading, or forfeiture, or any other unique form of punishment.

American states, though, still distinguish between felonies and misdemeanors. In the United States, the word "felony" typically indicates a crime that can get you more than a year of jail time, but each state is free to make its own definition. Maintaining a distinct category of serious crimes does occasionally come in handy. In the employment context, having a felony conviction on one's record may disqualify one from holding certain jobs (beautician in West Virginia) but not others (state senator in New York).

THE BIG H

. . . stands for **homicide**, a word that is often bandied about when discussion turns to felonies. The legal term for killing a person, it comes from the Latin *homo* (man) plus *caedere* (to slay).

THE
PARTY
OF THE
FIRST
PART

122

You may be surprised to learn that there is no crime called "homicide." It is simply an umbrella term that includes various types of **lawful homicide** as well as **unlawful homicide**. Before you dash off to settle a few old scores, however, it's worth noting that the categories of lawful homicide are awfully narrow.

One of them is **justifiable homicide**, which applies mainly to self-defense but can also apply to the defense of one's home from intruders. The latter is known as the **castle defense**, from the aphorism that "a man's house is his castle," a phrase first attributed to Sir Edward Coke in 1628. In such cases, the killing is intentional but "justified" by the circumstances. When the act of killing is truly unintentional, the law calls this **excusable homicide**. Despite the name, it is not enough to say "excuse me" to the victim in order to fit into this category. Rather, the defendant must show that the killing was accidental; for example, when a driver hits a pedestrian who ran into the street without warning. This category is also known as **homicide by misadventure**.

Murder comes from the Old English *mordor,* or *mord,* which first appears as a legal term around 1020 in the laws of King Cnut. This ancient term is said to have inspired the name "Mordor," the dark land of J.R.R. Tolkien's *Lord of the Rings*.

Mordor originally had a very narrow definition. It referred only to a secret or stealthy killing. Presumably the old sword-and-sandals crowd liked their killings done in full public view—remember, there was no TV—and so it was particularly unsporting to deny them this manly entertainment. By 1400, murder had evolved into its more modern sense of a deliberate killing. In the meantime, lawyers had dressed up *mordor* as a pseudo-Latin word: *murdrum*. From there, the word meandered back into English variously as *multrum, murdra, murtrum, murthrum,* and *murther*.

The archaic *murther* held its own well into the nineteenth century before yielding to murder. Thomas Jefferson, himself a lawyer, favored the older spelling, as in, "This Continental Congress sure is fun, but the paperwork is murther!"

The classic definition of murder, given by Coke in the seventeenth century, foreshadows many of the legal and linguistic complexities that have plagued this otherwise straightforward crime:

> When a person, of sound memory and discretion, unlawfully killeth any reasonable creature in being, and under the king's peace, with malice aforethought, either express or implied.

Of sound memory and discretion means sane. "Memory" here is being used as a synonym for mind, as was common in Elizabethan English. Another legacy of this usage is the common recital in a will (see Chapter 7) that "I, John Doe, being of sound mind and memory, do hereby make this will . . ." In these contexts, memory has nothing to do with the ability to recall past events.

A **reasonable creature** is not nearly so haughty as the Reasonable Man one keeps encountering in the law; rather, the term refers to any human. The additional words **in being** mean that the victim must have been born, thus touching on what even four hundred years ago was the hot-button topic of abortion. According to Coke's definition, abortion was not murder at common law.

THE
PARTY
OF THE
FIRST
PART

124

Malice aforethought is what Blackstone called the "grand criterion" of murder. In essence, it means that the killer had previously formed the intention to do the dastardly deed. Although pedantic types like to talk about **premeditated murder**, there is no crime by that name. Malice aforethought means that every murder, by definition, is premeditated.

The concept of malice is notoriously difficult for nonlawyers—a category that includes jury members. The ordinary definition of the word (from the Latin *malitia,* from *malus,* "bad") is hatred or spite. In criminal law, however, it is too restricting to require that all murderers act out of hatred. The man who poisons his rich uncle might plausibly argue that he bore no ill will toward the old fellow, he just wanted his inheritance. How could anyone prove otherwise?

Coke foresaw this problem by describing malice as being "either express or implied." By **implied malice**, Coke referred broadly to any deliberate action that brings about another's death. From the very beginning, therefore, malice aforethought has been, at best, a somewhat misleading way of saying that the killing wasn't a mere slip of the hand. It is still true today that a person can act with legal malice without being particularly malicious: A Tennessee jury instruction that was upheld by the Supreme Court in 1999 reassured the jury that they "need not be convinced that the defendant hated the person" that he killed.

In the case of an accidental killing, a court might still judge it to be "malicious" under the doctrine of **constructive malice**. Constructive malice is a component of the **felony murder rule**, which states that any homicide committed during the course of committing another felony will be considered murder. For example, if the driver of the getaway car from a jewel heist carelessly runs over and kills a pedestrian, the driver will be charged with murder rather than the lesser charge of manslaughter.

The word "**aforethought**," although very legal-sounding, adds almost nothing to the muddy malice requirement, except, perhaps, to exempt those killers who develop malicious thoughts only after bumping off their victims. Hardly one of the law's more pressing issues.

More importantly, "malice aforethought" begs the key question that has long bedeviled criminal law: How long *afore* the killing does the malice need to exist? An everyday quarrel can suddenly escalate; a person can decide to use deadly force a split second before he acts. Long ago, the law sought to exempt **crimes of passion** from murder—hot-blooded versus cold-blooded killing—by creating a doctrine with the jaunty name of **chance medley** ("medley" from the Old French *mesler*, to mix, and related to "meddle"). Although it sounds like an impromptu song, chance medley actually refers to a spontaneous brawl.

Killing someone in a chance medley was an early example of **manslaughter**, itself first recorded as a legal term in

1447, but in general use for many centuries before that. Manslaughter is a broad catchall, encompassing any sort of reckless or negligent act that causes death but where there was there was no intention to kill. Except when the killer was committing another felony, in which case he gets an upgrade to murder under the felony murder rule.

Today, the doctrine of chance medley has fallen into disuse, but the related defense of **provocation** still works. If you can show that your victim provoked you—basically, that he was asking for it—a court will reduce your murder charge to manslaughter. Not just any provocation will do; it has to be something that would lead our old friend, the Reasonable Man, to deadly violence.

As you will recall from Chapter 4, the Reasonable Man is not easily ruffled, but every man has his limit. The textbook case of provocation consists of one spouse finding the other spouse in bed with a lover (*she was in bed with that damn Collins again*), but other outrages may suffice (*and he was wearing my socks!*).

By the late eighteenth century, homicide was getting increasingly complicated. Blackstone identified no fewer than nine categories of homicide, all of them bearing hazy names like "chance medley" that gave little guidance to courts and lawyers. An altogether more systematic way to classify killing came from the state of Pennsylvania which, in 1794, passed the first law establishing **degrees** of murder—that is, subdividing murder according to levels of culpability. Virginia soon copied the idea, followed by other states. Before long, there were degrees of manslaughter as well.

If nothing else, degrees of crime have proven to be a

THE
PARTY
OF THE
FIRST
PART

126

boon to TV scriptwriters who delight in having steely-eyed prosecutors bark out "Man One!" during the inevitable **plea bargain** scene, in which the prosecutor offers to accept conviction for a lesser crime in return for an admission of guilt. The fictional **D.A.** (district attorney) will invariably accept nothing less than "Man One," which somehow sounds so much more *real* than "manslaughter in the first degree."

LEND ME YOUR EAR

After murder and manslaughter, the most serious felony in the common law was **mayhem**—a word that most people today think of as a general term for disorder—"it was mayhem at Filene's!" In fact, that usage became common only in the 1970s. Long before that, "mayhem" was a technical legal term. It still is.

Mayhem is the act of dismembering or disfiguring another person so as to weaken his ability to defend himself. It is a medieval term (surprise!) coming from the Anglo-Norman *maihem,* or injury. It was originally both a noun and a verb. Prosecutors would bring a charge of mayhem by stating that the defendant "feloniously did mayhem" the victim. By the latter part of the nineteenth century, the verb form gave way to the closely related **maim**.

One is tempted to ask: Wouldn't *any* dismemberment weaken one's defenses? Well, that's not the way the law sees it. Traditionally, it was mayhem to chop off a limb, but not an ear or a nose, because, as Blackstone blandly put it, "they can be of no use in fighting." Indeed, even loss of limb did not deter some plucky combatants, as Monty

Python's Black Knight demonstrates: *Come back, I'll bite your legs off!*

Mayhem is now an obsolete term in England and in United States federal law, where the last traces of it were removed in 1961. It is alive and well, however, in the statutes of many American states. Massachusetts has the crime of mayhem, but in a welcome relaxation of the common law, the crime includes chopping off a nose or an ear. Mississippi's mayhem law explicitly includes the loss of a nose, but is silent about the ear.

THE
PARTY
OF THE
FIRST
PART

128

ASSAULT AND PEPPER

Which brings us to that great double-barreled category **assault and battery**: two words that routinely confuse non-lawyers. In the common law, an "assault" refers only to *threats* of violence, not the violence itself. If blows are actually landed, then the law calls it a battery, which as we saw in Chapter 4 is exactly how the word is used in tort, so at least there's some consistency. Think of it this way: You can have an assault without a battery, but you can't have a battery without an assault, since every physical attack is preceded by some sort of threatening gesture—the windup to the punch if nothing else.

The problem is that plain English never restricted "assaults" to mere threats; the word has been used for centuries to describe any sort of onslaught. Add to that the fact that "battery" in the sense of beating went out of fashion around the eighteenth century, and you have a clear case of legal language running off the rails of plain English.

The confusion over these terms is legendary. Legislators

throughout the common law world have attempted, with varying degrees of success, to reform the language of assault and battery. In Britain, these crimes have been merged into a single offense called **common assault**, but since the statute actually uses the word "battery" to define common assault, this is hardly a victory for Plain English. Adding to the confusion, Britain has separate offenses for causing **Actual Bodily Harm** and the more serious **Grievous Bodily Harm**, or **GBH**, as lawyers call it.

The infinite gradations of human violence do not, of course, fit neatly into these pseudoprecise categories. The Crown Prosecution Service—the department responsible for prosecuting crimes in Britain—has frankly conceded that the terms are fuzzy. On their website, they cheerfully observe that an "un-displaced broken nose" could be either common assault or actual bodily harm. But if *they* don't know, who does?

Some American states, such as Texas, have a single crime of "assault" that also includes common law battery. In other states, "assault" now refers to what the common law called battery, while a new crime of **menacing** takes the place of common law assault. Many states now have degrees of assault. The most serious is **first degree assault** ("Ass One!"), which in some states has replaced common law mayhem. The result of all this linguistic creativity is that the average American citizen has no idea what "assault" means in his or her state: A threat? An attack? Both?

Surely the courts have the answer. The place to look is the magisterial treatise *Words and Phrases,* which contains thousands of summaries of cases in which courts have defined legal terms, including assault and battery. Should you have a free weekend and several hogsheads of coffee, a thorough study of *Words and Phrases* will yield the following pearls:

- Assault is an attempt or threat to do bodily harm and does not mean a battery.
- A battery is an assault.
- The term "assault" in the federal act included the offense defined as "battery" in the Illinois statute.
- Assault [includes] an unlawful touching with criminal intent.
- [T]here is no touching of a victim in an assault.
- The inmate allegedly threw cartons of . . . urine, milk and feces onto the passing guard, spat on the guard, and threatened the guard, but nothing suggested conduct rose to the level of assault.
- Abusive throwing of any liquid onto [a] correction officer constitutes assault.
- Assault has two meanings at common law.
- There are three recognized definitions of assault.
- The term "battery" is one of common usage and understanding.

What's more, each state's penal code is crowded with subcategories of assault and battery. Generally, these laws were passed in the heat of the moment to deal with a particular outrage. In one state or another, the legislature has seen fit to outlaw **assaulting a schoolteacher**, **assaulting a healthcare worker**, and even **assaulting a police horse**.

The names of some of these crimes have a distinctly regional flavor. Assault and battery committed by multiple

THE
PARTY
OF THE
FIRST
PART

130

assailants is **lynching** in South Carolina and Mississippi, while in New York it would be a **gang assault**.

On a related note, "lynching" comes from the term **lynch law**—essentially any self-proclaimed law—but the origin of lynch law is anybody's guess. Some say it is named for Charles Lynch, a justice of the peace in eighteenth-century Virginia who took it upon himself to summarily imprison suspected Tories. Others give the honors to Captain William Lynch, also a Virginian from the colonial period. Still others say the term comes from Lynch's Creek in South Carolina, where an early vigilante group used to gather.

SHANGHAI CRIMES AND MISDEMEANORS

Another legal term from the New World is **kidnapping**, the forcible abduction of a person against his will. "Kidnapper" was coined in the seventeenth century to describe those who snatched people to labor in the plantations of colonial America. Despite its name, kidnapping has nothing to do with children—"kid" was an old expression for an indentured servant. The word "indenture," as you may recall from Chapter 2, is related to teeth. The *nap* in kidnap is more mysterious—possibly Dutch or Scandinavian; it has nothing to do with getting forty winks, but rather seems to be related to the better-known "nab."

One of the most notorious forms of kidnapping was the practice of forcing men to serve on ships, which was often the only way to get people to undergo the misery of a long voyage. In the United States, the official name of this crime is **Shanghaiing Sailors** (Title 18, Section 2194 of the

U.S. Code, if you don't believe me). The verb "to shanghai" is recorded as early as 1871, but was probably in use well before then in the western United States. Most likely the phrase was inspired by the fact that Shanghai was a common destination in those days of booming Asian trade. In port cities like San Francisco and Portland, professional kidnappers known as **crimps** (an English word of uncertain origin) would conscript vulnerable young men, often after plying them with alcohol—perhaps a Singapore Sling?—or opium, or both.

THE
PARTY
OF THE
FIRST
PART

132

TAKE MY PROPERTY—PLEASE

The last of our major felonies, **theft** is an Anglo-Saxon word meaning "taking another's goods." **Larceny**, a Latinate term for theft, can be traced to an English law of 1225 that sought to punish those who stole deer from the royal hunting parks. The crime was given the name *latrocinium,* later anglicized to latrociny and finally larceny. The next larceny statute came fifty years later and was also, bizarrely, limited to the theft of the King's deer. Could it be that for fifty years the British Crown had no more pressing business than to crack down on deer theft?

Be that as it may, larceny was quickly subdivided into two categories: **grand** and **petit** (sometimes spelled **petty**). **Petit larceny** applied when the value of the goods stolen was less than twelve pence; when the value was greater, it was **grand larceny** and the penalty was death.

That was all well and good in the Middle Ages, but what with inflation and all, hanging a man for stealing thirteen pence began to look a little harsh in the early nineteenth century. Judges, however, refused to alter the common law definition of grand larceny, and it became something of an embarrassment as men were sent to the gallows for stealing trifling amounts. One English wit, Sir Henry Spelman, blithely noted that while everything else became dearer, a man's life kept getting cheaper. The ancient definition of grand larceny remained valid in America until at least 1815 and in England until 1827.

When businessmen steal from the till, they are usually accused of **embezzlement** (from Anglo-French *enbesiler,* "to carry off"). Embezzlement—the pilfering of goods that one has lawful, but temporary, possession of—was originally aimed at light-fingered servants in English country houses. There had been a gap in the law: theft by a servant did not fit the technical definition of larceny because the servant did not *initially* gain possession of the goods illegally. The butler, for example, was perfectly entitled to handle the silver for the purpose of polishing it. Unfortunately, he sometimes forgot to put it back.

Contrary to popular belief, **robbery** (from the Old French term for stealing, *roberie*) is not the same thing as theft. Rather, it is theft committed in the presence of the victim—a holdup. The common phrase **highway robbery** actually began life as a technical legal term: it was a robbery committed on the King's highway. Those who committed the crime, known as **highwaymen**, were more severely punished than other robbers. It was only in the twentieth century that "highway robbery" became a metaphor for excessive fees or charges.

Burglary, as we saw in the Collins case, is unlawful entry with the intent of committing a crime within the place entered. It appears that "burglary" originally referred to the breach of a walled town rather than an individual house. The "burg" in "burglary" is most likely related to words like **borough** and **burgh**. The use of deadly force against a burglar is often justifiable; after all, a burgher's home is his White Castle.

BOOK 'EM

All of this talk about criminal law is purely hypothetical unless the State has some method to catch and prosecute criminals. This is the realm of **criminal procedure**.

THE
PARTY
OF THE
FIRST
PART

134

The vocabulary of criminal procedure is striking in its reliance on highfalutin Latin terms. If you find yourself accused of committing a crime, your first punishment will be a barrage of ancient Roman verbiage. Some of the more common ones:

habeas corpus
corpus delicti
subpoena
nolo contendere
nolle prosequi
billa vera

Most of this Latin was introduced into English law by William the Conqueror, the Norman invader who seized England in 1066. William—a bit of a control freak, truth be told—refused to allow legal business to be conducted in English, which was then a jumble of dialects with anarchic spellings. Instead he required writs and statutes to be in Latin, a thoroughly standardized language, guaranteed to be the same from Canterbury to York.

William's system left English judges with a tradition of demanding perfect schoolboy Latin in court documents. In 1533, one convicted murderer was spared the gallows because the Latin indictment contained the word *quidam* instead of *quidem*. A hundred years later, another case was reversed because the writ to the sheriff misspelled *praecipimus* ("we command") as *praecipipimus,* even though there was no ambiguity about what was meant.

Habeas corpus is probably the most famous example of legal Latin. It was originally a means of challenging the legality of a prisoner's detention. The words literally mean "You have the body," which was a shorthand way of saying, "you have the body, so bring him to court and we'll decide whether he ought to be detained." It is still an official term in American and British law. When the young defense lawyer says "I'm bringing a habeas motion," it means that he thinks the police are holding a prisoner on trumped-up charges.

Somewhat confusingly, criminal procedure also requires a **corpus delicti** (the "body of the crime"), where *corpus* refers not to a human body but to the "body of evidence." *Corpus delicti* is nothing more than evidence that a crime took place. Almost inevitably, the term gets confused with "corpse," especially since a corpse happens to be first-rate evidence of a crime. The *corpus delicti,* however, need not be a corpse; any evidence will do.

A *subpoena* (literally, "under penalty"), as we saw in Chapter 3, is a document used to compel a witness to testify, the full name being **subpoena ad testificandum**. It can also be used to order a person to hand over evidence, in which case it is called a **subpoena duces tecum,** Latin for "bring it with you or else."

In 1731, the English Parliament came tantalizingly close to banning the use of Latin phrases like *habeas corpus* and *corpus delicti*. In that year, the House of Commons passed a law prohibiting Latin, French, and all other foreign languages in legal proceedings. Here was an invitation presented to British lawyers on a silver platter with watercress around the edges. They could finally embrace the language of their clients without fear of being professionally disadvantaged. It was a gigantic leap toward plain language in the law.

THE
PARTY
OF THE
FIRST
PART

136

What happened? The legal establishment bellowed its protests from the highest courts to the lowest. Lord Raymond, then the Chief Justice of England, saw no end to the horrors. Why, if lawyers were allowed to speak English, they might just as well speak *Welsh*. (In fact it was not until 1942 that people were allowed to speak the Welsh language in Welsh courts.) By 1733, a chastened Parliament passed an amendment that allowed lawyers to continue to use "technical words" and other "commonly used" terms in foreign languages.

This amendment created a loophole through which one could drive a Hummer, since any foreign word in the mouth of an English lawyer could be said to be "technical" or "commonly used," or both. This ingenious method of appearing to renounce Latin while doing nothing of the sort has influenced legal writing ever since. The *Style Manual* for the New York State Court System (2002), for example, declares that the use of Latin in court papers is "discouraged," but then immediately grants an exception for any Latin word or phrase that is a "legal term of art."

The usual justification for clinging to Latin is that phrases like *habeas corpus* sound silly if translated into English. "I'm bringing a you-have-the-body motion" just doesn't have the force of "I'm bringing a habeas motion." But this argument assumes, again, that word-for-word translation is the only option, which is the kind of logic that fills one with constructive malice. In fact, good English synonyms for habeas corpus already exist: It has been called the **writ of liberty** and the **Great Writ**, both of which are perfectly good English phrases. Or one could come up with a new name for habeas corpus; call it a "custody challenge motion" or an "anti-detention motion." Just like teacher says: *Use your words.*

To be fair, this is beginning to happen, at least in Britain. Almost three hundred years after Lord Raymond went to the barricades in defense of Latin, another Chief Justice, Lord Woolf, finally took up the cause of plain language. In 1999, thanks to lobbying by the Plain English Campaign and others, Woolf succeeded in largely banning Latin phrases from Britain's civil courts. By 2002, similar efforts to excise Latin from the criminal courts were under way. For common Latin expressions, Woolf provided plain English equivalents, things like "in private" instead of *in camera* and "advocate to the court" rather than *amicus curiae*—much to the dismay, one imagines, of his high school Latin teacher.

No end of English lawyers and judges have got their knickers in a frightful twist over the whole affair. One lawyer, John Gray, peevishly wrote in the introduction to his book *Lawyers' Latin*: "To attempt suppression of Latin in a civilized country is, in the scale of cultural atrocities, on a par with burning books."

As recently as 2004, Roderick Munday, an Oxford law don, dismissed Woolf's reforms as a shoddy bit of "legal 'PR.'" In a lengthy article, Munday describes the legal profession's "bewilderment at the willful and, to a great degree, pointless impoverishment of the vocabulary of the English law." Yes, yes, it is a shame to have to use words that the general public might understand, but then, *sic biscuitis disintegrat* (that's the way the cookie crumbles).

That Lord Woolf's reforms have led to such *anni horribili* for the bar simply proves that lawyers continue to speak Latin as a matter of preference, not because they are compelled to do so. After all, it is exceedingly rare that a lawyer is called upon to represent an ancient Roman in a twenty-first-century courtroom. Yet Latin remains as one of the most durable badges of exclusivity in the legal profession.

THE
PARTY
OF THE
FIRST
PART

138

Lawyers even go to the trouble of turning perfectly good English words into Latin, as we saw earlier with *murdrum*. Another example is the phrase **quo warranto** (by what warrant?), which is the name of a legal procedure used to challenge a government official's authority. The word *warranto* was made up by adding an *o* to the English "warrant." This sort of reverse etymology is known as "back-formation," and it is really no better than the tendency of some people to add an *o* to the ends of words to make them sound Italian or Spanish ("Rodolfo, turn on the computer-o, I want to surf the Web-o.")

CRIMINAL SLANGUAGE

Oddly enough, as soon as a criminal case gets to court, legal language goes from archaic formality to the other extreme—slang. Something about the conveyer-belt rapidity of criminal justice demands a looser way of speaking.

Criminal law slang is very much a local invention; it changes from country to country and even from city to city. Thus, a British prosecutor might offer a witness immunity in return for **Q.E.**, or "turning Queen's evidence"; in New York, such an arrangement would be known as a **queen-for-a-day agreement** (the two queens are not related), while in Washington, D.C., it is called an **immunity bath**. In some American states, if a prosecutor wants to chat with a suspected criminal, but isn't ready to commit to an immunity deal, he'll send a **Mae West letter**, as in "Come up and see me sometime."

When a prosecutor decides not to pursue a possible charge, he **no-papers** the case. Another way of saying the same thing is to enter a **nol pros**, short for the Latin *nolle prosequi* ("to be unwilling to pursue"), also known as a **nolle** (pronounced "nolly"). This is not to be confused with entering a **nolo**, which is what the defendant pleads if he does not dispute the charges brought against him. "Nolo" is short for *nolo contendere* ("I do not contest"), and some courts have thoughtfully updated the name of this plea to "no contest." The advantage of a nolo plea—as distinct from a plain guilty plea—is that it cannot be used against the defendant in a later civil lawsuit (see Chapter 3 for more on those).

Some slang terms have been around so long they aren't even considered slang. The word **culprit**, for example, is a very old piece of slang. In the Middle Ages, the official records of criminal cases used to begin with the words *culpabilis: prest* (the latter related to the French *prêt,* or "ready"), meaning "the prosecution says he is guilty and is ready to prove it." Court clerks began to abbreviate the phrase as *culp: prest* and then *culp: prit*. Ultimately it morphed into the compact noun we use today.

The use of criminal law slang often degenerates into what linguists call **telegraphic speech**—that is, highly condensed utterances. This is the language of toddlers and of newspaper headlines, most of which would be incomprehensible without the relevant background: "Bulls Smash Pistons!" "Madonna and Child in Car Chase!" or "Hill Jabs Bush!"

One can often hear telegraphic speech just outside the courtroom as prosecutors and defense lawyers try to cut deals. New York lawyers Glen Murray and Gary Muldoon have catalogued this sort of language in their engaging *Criminal Slanguage of New York*. Using Murray and Muldoon's vocabulary, a telegraphic exchange in a New York courthouse might sound something like this:

THE
PARTY
OF THE
FIRST
PART

140

SLANG	TRANSLATION
Prosecutor: We've got your client on IBC with a prior mal mish.	*Your client is charged with issuing bad checks, and has a previous conviction for malicious mischief.*
Defense lawyer: How about a plea? We'd take GL2 with a two bullet cap.	*The defendant would plead guilty to Second Degree Grand Larceny, if the prosecutor will agree to a 2-year maximum sentence.*
Prosecutor: Man One!	*First Degree Manslaughter!*
Defense lawyer: What the hell are you talking about?	
Prosecutor: I don't know, I just like the sound of that.	

Suspected criminals must be formally charged in writing. In the case of felonies, the written accusation is known as an **indictment**.

Nonlawyers often misspell "indict" because it is actually pronounced "indite." That may not seem terribly unusual—English is full of silent letters like the "c" in indict—but lawyers actually went out of their way to make the word unphonetic. The word used to be spelled just as it was spoken: *indite*. Some long-forgotten seventeenth-century lawyer thought that adding a *c* would make the word look more like its Latin ancestor *indictare*. Interescting.

An indictment will have one or more **counts**, or criminal charges. When used in this sense, "count" is derived from the French *conte* (story or narrative) and is related to the verb recount, as in "he recounted a delightful story." In old English practice, courtroom lawyers were called *counters,* or in Latin *narratores*—they told a story.

In the United States, an indictment is **handed down** by a **grand jury**. "Grand" is used here in the French sense of big, since a grand jury traditionally had twenty-three members rather than twelve. In medieval times, accusatory evidence was written on documents called "bills of indictment." If the grand jury thought that the evidence merited a trial, they would write *billa vera* (true bill) on the back of the bill. To this day, grand jurors vote for a **true bill** when they opt to indict a suspect.

Which they invariably do, according to aggrieved defense lawyers. So common are grand jury indictments that it has become an American ritual for criminal defense

lawyers to stand on the courthouse steps—cameras
rolling—and declare with indignation:

> My client is perfectly innocent! Everyone knows
> that **a grand jury will indict a ham sandwich.**

The sandwich metaphor is a shorthand protest against the
perceived unfairness of the grand jury system. Certain
procedural quirks—like the fact that defense counsel is
not permitted to appear, and that the prosecutor has no
obligation to make a balanced presentation—are thought
to guarantee an indictment against just about anybody
the local prosecutor wants to indict, even certain food-
stuffs.

Most authorities agree that the first person to make the
ham sandwich joke was Sol Wachtler, then–Chief Judge of
New York's highest court, in a 1985 interview. In what
can safely be called an ironic twist, Wachtler himself was
indicted seven years later for harassing his former mistress,
a New York socialite. Perhaps he felt vindicated in his earlier disparagement of grand juries; however, there is no
record that Wachtler stood on the courthouse steps and repeated his ham-sandwich zinger.

Wachtler was convicted and sentenced to serve time. Because he was diagnosed with a severe mental illness, he was
ultimately referred for psychiatric treatment at Rochester
Prison, a federal facility associated with the Mayo Clinic.
The moral of the story, I suppose, is that even if a ham sandwich is indicted, it still gets Mayo.

THE
PARTY
OF THE
FIRST
PART

142

Speaking of mental illness, the **insanity defense** is one of the few reliable means for an otherwise guilty person to avoid time in **jail** (or, in England, **gaol**—in both cases from the Norman French word for birdcage, *gaiole*). The bad news, as Judge Wachtler could attest, is that the defendant has to go to a state mental institution, so it isn't necessarily much of a step up.

Although the insanity defense is often thought of as a concession to modern theories of mental hygiene, it is actually an ancient doctrine based on the belief, as Blackstone so delicately put it, that "lunatics or infants . . . are incapable of committing any crime." In Blackstone's day, acquitted lunatics were locked up in a hospital called St. Mary of Bethlehem, popularly known as **Bedlam**, which has since come to be a general expression for confusion.

ARRESTING
LANGUAGE

143

The best-known test throughout the English-speaking world for legal insanity is the **M'Naghten Test**, which comes from the 1843 trial of Daniel M'Naghten, a mad Englishman who killed the prime minister's secretary, Edward Drummond. A panel of judges came up with a definitive test of insanity: No man shall be criminally responsible if he was "laboring under such a defect of reason . . . as not to know the nature and quality of the act he was doing; or . . . that he did not know what he was doing was wrong."

Most states still recognize the M'Naghten Test. Its longevity probably owes much to the flexibility of its language—terms like "defect of reason" are as empty as "malice aforethought." Over time, the law has supplemented M'Naghten with tests for **temporary insanity**, which go by such vivid names as the **irresistible impulse test** and the **wild beast test**. Some states also recognize a less severe form of mental impairment called **diminished capacity**—sometimes referred to as the **Twinkie Defense** after an infamous 1979 trial in which defense lawyers convinced a jury that a killer's rational judgment had been impaired by eating sugary junk food.

The proliferation of insanity defenses has led many to denounce the whole concept as a too-convenient technicality for criminals. Ambrose Bierce in his *Devil's Dictionary* (1911), for example, defined **sanity** as "a state of mind which immediately precedes and follows murder." But the law in all its strictness takes seriously the need to judge each person individually. As the philosophers say, you never know what a person suffers until you walk a mile in his shoes. Or socks, as the case may be.

THE
PARTY
OF THE
FIRST
PART

144

7

WILLS, WIVES, AND WRECKS

Mystic Testament: A will under seal.

— SHUMAKER AND LONGSDORF,
THE CYCLOPEDIC LAW DICTIONARY

The Nobel Prize–winning playwright George Bernard Shaw did not live long enough to see his play *Pygmalion* turned into the smash Broadway musical *My Fair Lady*. But his heirs did. Seven years after Shaw's death in 1950, they were still fighting over his will.

Not that there was any real doubt about the meaning of Shaw's will. His clear, albeit eccentric, wish was that the bulk of his small fortune would go into a **charitable trust** to encourage the development of a phonetic English alphabet that might someday replace the familiar twenty-six-letter version.

The problem was the language of Shaw's will. His lawyer had written the original document, but Shaw couldn't resist adding a few of his own colorful paragraphs to the otherwise bland testament. He went on and on about the new alphabet, specifying that it must have no fewer than forty characters, including sixteen vowels—and even that, he lamented, "does not pretend to be exhaustive." He harangued against phoneticians and inventors of "rival alphabets" who had stood in the way of real reform. And he urged that some of the money from the trust be used for "advertisement and propaganda" in support of the proposed alphabet.

In the minds of lawyers, Shaw's unconventional language created an opportunity to attack the will—after all, a will that is interesting to read can't possibly be legally valid. Shaw's heirs, frustrated at the prospect of all those royalties going toward a crackpot scheme, challenged the validity of the charitable trust. Eventually, the case came up for trial before Mr. Justice Harman, who made not the slightest effort to hide his disdain for Shaw's attempt to play the lawyer. He scolded the deceased playwright for failing to control his *cacoethes scribendi* (itch for writing) and for upsetting the "delicate testamentary machinery" that Shaw's lawyer had created.

Harman declared that the alphabet trust failed to qualify as a **charity**—and here the judge pointed out that the "lawyer's sense" of the word "charity" quite often "excludes benevolent or philanthropic activities which the layman would consider charitable." Whereas most people would have considered research and education to be a charitable endeavor, it had to be "beneficial" in the eyes of the law before it could be declared a charity. And there was no consensus from the outset that Shaw's alphabet would be beneficial; Shaw's own annotations to the will proved that even he realized it would be controversial.

And so Harman invalidated the alphabet trust—all because one of the greatest writers in the English language had had the nerve to add some of *his own* words to *his own* will. The judge's parting shot was "It is not the fault of the law, but of the **testator** [Shaw]."

The lawyers who write wills and the judges who interpret them are, to put it mildly, obsessed with preserving ancient formalities. Thousands of cases have been decided on the tiniest punctilio of procedure. To give just one example: A California court once invalidated a will because the date at the top was partly handwritten and partly printed—it had to be all one or the other.

It is this kind of thinking that makes the language of wills the most conservative in the legal lexicon. It is a beacon for those who long to **bequeath their chattels real to the aforesaid residuary legatees**, but somewhat less illuminating for the rest of us.

In almost every instance, lawyers defend this linguistic conservatism as being necessary to prevent a **will contest**—not a competition to see who can write the best will, but litigation over the meaning of the will itself. It is an article of faith among lawyers who write wills that rigid adherence to words and phrases that have survived for centuries will lead to less ambiguity and therefore fewer will contests.

It is a noble goal. Will contests and other sorts of probate litigation are notoriously long and expensive. The worst was undoubtedly the British case of *Jennings* v. *Jennings,* which inspired the fictional *Jarndyce* v. *Jarndyce* in Charles Dickens's *Bleak House.* The Jennings case began in 1798 and did not reach a conclusion until 1878. That's not a typo; the case languished in the courts for *eighty years.* The final result: Every penny of the Jennings estate went to pay legal fees.

As for Shaw's will, Justice Harman's ruling led to an out-of-court settlement that allowed only a small portion of Shaw's estate to go to the alphabet trust. In 1959, a linguist named Walter Kingsley Read won a contest (but not a will contest) to design the alphabet; his creation was a shorthand-looking script known as Shavian (the adjective form of Shaw). It has thus far proved to have no practical or literary use. All the same, it's nice to have an alternative alphabet in case of emergencies.

SAY WHAT?

One can hardly fault lawyers for trying to ensure that wills and related documents are written clearly. Unfortunately, the language that they have chosen for the task is about as obscure as—well, Shavian.

THE
PARTY
OF THE
FIRST
PART

148

Consider the following notice, which, although it sounds like one of Charles Dickens's parodies, was actually filed in an American probate court in 1993 (the names have been changed):

NOTICE OF FILING OF ACCOUNT

The accounting of John Doe, Dative Ancillary Testamentary Executor of the Succession of Jane D. Roe, also known as Jane Doris Roe, covering the period from January 1, 1988 through December 31, 1992 has been filed. The account may be homologated after the expiration of ten days from the date on which this notice is mailed. A copy of the account is attached.

Anytown, USA, this 20th day of August, 1993.

By: Peter Poe
    Attorney for John Doe, Dative Ancillary Testamentary Executor

Now imagine the expectant nephew, eagerly sifting through the court records to figure out how much old Aunt Jane was really worth. Would this document help him? Most likely he'd glaze right over it. If he bothered to read it, he'd be left wondering what exactly happens when a court **homologates** the **accounting** of a **dative ancillary testamentary executor**.

In fact, this document will point the nephew to what he is looking for. It is saying that the executor of Ms. Roe's estate has filed an official inventory of the estate's assets and liabilities—in short, the loot.

The **executor** is the person responsible for making sure

that the will gets carried out. Without going into too much detail, all the stuff about "dative blah blah blah" basically means that the executor was appointed by a court rather than named in the will, a fact that is totally irrelevant for the purposes of the notice. The bit about homologation means that the executor is asking the court to approve the inventory.

One hates to throw cold water on a well-meaning lawyer, and, to be fair, it isn't every day that one's accounting gets homologated, but this notice could have been written in plain English—hell, in *English*—without any risk of ambiguity.

THE
PARTY
OF THE
FIRST
PART

150

LEGALESE IS FOREVER

At least one law professor, Stanley Johanson of the University of Texas, is doing something to reform the language of wills. As a classroom exercise, he subjects traditional wills to a readability analysis, the aptly named Fog Index. The higher the index, the less readable the document. Popular magazines usually score around 12 on the Fog Index. Anything over 40 is considered entirely too foggy for most people to understand.

Johanson shows his students that conventionally written wills typically score in the high 40s or above. That sets the stage for teaching the principles of plain-English drafting, including the sage advice that "the will should be expressed in language that people, as distinguished from lawyers, regularly employ. . . . Legal jargon should not be resorted to except when absolutely necessary."

Remarkably—and yet, somehow, predictably— Johanson's teaching methods have landed him in controversy. In his 2002 article (see Chapter 2), Professor David

Crump takes Johanson to task for encouraging "an unex-amined preference for something called plain English."

Crump argues that Johanson and other plain-language advocates fail to recognize that there are two categories of legal documents: **persuasion documents** and **preservation documents**. According to Crump, plain English will do for persuasion documents, which are intended to make a quick point, but not for preservation documents, which are needed for long-term purposes. The latter must be written with formal legal jargon, even if it means "polysyl-labics shrouded by a high Fog Index." Poor Professor Jo-hanson: He must be kicking himself for missing that boat.

The distinctly alarming upshot of Crump's theory is that the documents we plan to keep the longest—the ones we lovingly pack up in archival vaults and safe deposit boxes—are supposed to be the least comprehensible ones. And that includes wills. A will need not be written in plain English, writes Crump, because it "will not be rou-tinely read by someone who needs to understand it." The logical rejoinder, of course, is that a will needs to be read and understood *at least once.*

In any event, Crump muddies up his own theory by in-troducing a third category of **hybrid documents** that are part plain, part precise. And then he goes on to say, "In a sense, all documents are hybrid documents." An odd con-cession, one might think, for a champion of precision.

WHERE THERE'S A WILL, THERE'S A TESTAMENT

If Crump's theory has any validity at all, then it must mean that the hypertechnical language of wills is necessary to "preserve" some precise meaning. Really? Let's start right at the top of the document. A **last will and testament** is what lawyers call a document by which a person may **give, devise and bequeath** his or her estate. A lot of words just to leave your collection of souvenir spoons to Cousin Ethel.

If you consult a lawyer, you will probably be told that every syllable of those archaic phrases has a distinct meaning. A **will**, for example, is typically defined by lawyers as a document used for making gifts of real property (land and buildings). The verb one must use when giving away real property is "**to devise.**" A **testament**, according to ancient authorities, is a document that can only be used for disposing of personal property (stuff other than land). The verb for giving away personal property is "**to bequeath.**"

Now—the scales falling from your eyes—you finally see the elegance of legal language. There are no wasted words. We have a perfectly logical system in which one can *devise* land using a *will* and *bequeath* goods via a *testament*. The law has very thoughtfully combined these two great concepts into one convenient document: the last will and testament.

Unfortunately, it's all a load of hooey.

No matter how many lawyers regurgitate the traditional explanations, scholars have proven that the distinction between "will" and "testament" was made up out of whole cloth in a vain attempt to make sense out of what is essentially meaningless excess verbiage.

As a legal term, **will** is directly related to the common auxiliary verb "will," as in "I will go to the store today." In Anglo-Saxon times, there was no legal mechanism to guarantee the disposition of one's property after death. The most one could do was to draft a document stating one's desire, or

THE
PARTY
OF THE
FIRST
PART

152

as they said in Old English, *ic wille* ("I desire") that, for example, Ethelbert should have my axe, Ethelred my sword, and so on. These documents became known as "wills," and over time they became legally binding.

Meanwhile, in the ecclesiastical courts, a similar type of document had developed that was known by the Latin name **testamentum**, or **testament**. It was in the fifteenth and sixteenth centuries—a period when English lawyers were in a state of perpetual confusion as to which language they should use—that the two words got together in the immortal phrase "last will and testament."

Originally, last will and testament was a deliberate redundancy: saying the same thing in two languages just to be clear. But lawyers soon applied their conventional rules of interpretation, which presume that different words in the same document must have distinct meanings. Sir Edward Coke was one of many lawyers to subscribe to the frivolous distinction between wills and testaments.

And as for calling your will the "last will," just think about that for a minute. What does it prove? Every will you write is your last—until you write the next one. If there are two wills left in the safe after you die, it would defy logic to give one of them priority simply because it said "last will" at the top.

In a British case from 1890, a man named Van Cutsem had written a document titled "last will" but then later wrote another will, obviously meant to replace will No. 1, but lacking the words "last will." The court decided that the first will, being the "last will," had somehow been intended to revoke the second will. Odd—but then this was the age that produced H. G. Wells's *The Time Machine,* which was published five years later.

Even today, these pseudoprecise words can create ambiguity. Not long ago I downloaded a will off the Internet; it proudly bears the title "Last Will and Testament." Several paragraphs in, the document says that it "revokes all Wills and **Codicils** [an amendment to a will] previously made," but says nothing about revoking earlier testaments. What became of the former testaments? Will they ever get homologated?

The fact is that no law actually requires the use of the phrase "last will and testament"—lawyers repeat these words out of habit, provoking judges, as in the Van Cutsem case, to confer upon them meanings that were never intended. Unless you're trying to impress people—and after you're dead, who cares?—you can just call the thing a "will" and be done with it.

THE
PARTY
OF THE
FIRST
PART

154

'TIS BETTER TO GIVE
THAN TO BEQUEATH

"Give, devise, and bequeath" has a nice ring to it, as though your heirs will get your vintage cuff links three times over, but there is no point in using this phrase in a post-jousting world.

Both *give* and *bequeath* come from Anglo-Saxon, while *devise* is an Old French term. As with will and testament, cautious lawyers thought it best to lump these words together into one polyglot phrase. Later generations of lawyers developed the bogus theory that one can *devise* only realty, whereas one must *bequeath* personalty. It was never quite clear what one was supposed to *give*—blood, perhaps?

In 1945, a Kansas lawyer tried to convince a court that

a man who drafted a will "didn't have any legal knowledge because he used the word *'bequeath'* in devising real property and the word *'devise'* in bequeathing personal property." Which is, of course, the kind of slur that besmirches a family's reputation for generations. In 1953, a New York court was asked to interpret a provision in a will in which the testator states, "I give, devise and bequeath to my trustee" certain property "consisting of real estate." Notwithstanding the bit about "real estate," the court held that the testator must have intended the trustee to inherit personal property as well—why else would he have used the word "bequeath"?

Nowadays, the legal profession is a little bit more relaxed—even indiscriminate—in using these terms. That will I got off the Internet, for example, contains the classic "give, devise and bequeath" in two places. In another clause the phrase is altered to "will, give and bequeath," a somewhat unusual use of will as a transitive verb. In another section, property is just "given," and in yet another, the testator has the temerity to suggest that real property can be bequeathed. Heretic!

So give your heirs a break; don't "devise" or "bequeath" your stuff. Just *give* it.

COWS AND OTHER PROPERTY

The property that one gives and devises and bequeaths is known as the **decedent's estate** or simply **estate** (related to the Latin *status*). It's the stuff that the person owned at the time of his or her death. Likewise, the property left over after a business "dies" is known as the **bankruptcy estate**.

The job of a will is to get rid of the estate. Many wills

start the ball rolling with a number of **specific bequests**—that is, a certain thing goes to a certain person. For example, you might write:

"To Wanita, my recipe for chocolate chip cookies," or "To Kristopher, my artificial vagina."

But why not make the beneficiary sweat a little? After all, it's your party. Many wills contain **conditional bequests**, otherwise known as **conditional gifts**. That means that the beneficiary gets the gift only if a specific condition is fulfilled. So, for example, you could say:

"To Judge Harman, my Rolls-Royce, provided he writes all his judgments in Shavian."

Conditional gifts can be wonderfully capricious. Men and women often leave their spouses with a steady income, provided they never remarry. A surprising number of fathers in the late nineteenth and early twentieth centuries left money to their sons on the condition that the sons not grow mustaches. One retired schoolteacher in England left £26,000 in trust to be paid to Jesus Christ, but only if the Second Coming were to occur within eighty years of the teacher's death. There are still about fifty years to go on this condition, so it is impossible to say for certain whether the inducement will work.

Specific bequests call for clear language—say exactly what you want to give and to whom you want to give it. Unfortunately, traditional wills have a way of obscuring the best of intentions. Individual items are often lumped together as "**goods and chattels**," a phrase with legal overtones but no clear definition. "Good" is an English word, related to the Old Norse *gothr*. "Chattels" comes from the

THE
PARTY
OF THE
FIRST
PART

156

Latin *catalla,* which literally means cattle but in Old French came to mean any moveable good—which is an odd usage, given that cattle are notoriously difficult to move.

And then there is **said**—or even worse, **aforesaid**. These words came into English as the equivalents of the Latin *dictus* (said) and *predictus* (aforesaid). There's a certain *gravitas,* if you will, about these words that makes otherwise sensible men mindlessly parrot them. Why leave money to your favorite nephews and nieces when you can leave it to "the aforesaid nephews and nieces"? It sounds so much more sophisticated! That's exactly what one Englishman did in his will; the problem was that he forgot to name any nieces or nephews anywhere in his will, so his erudite "aforesaid" had no antecedent. A judge decided that the estate would therefore have to go to *all* of the nieces and nephews, whether their uncle liked them or not.

THE LEFTOVERS

Once the specific bequests are paid out, anything that remains is referred to as the **rest, residue, and remainder** of the testator's estate: the final blast of legalese in many wills. This phrase emerged from a prolonged struggle among lawyers to find just the right words to describe the leftover bits of one's estate. In the fourteenth century, **residue and remnant** was popular down at probate court. By the sixteenth century, **rest and residue** was all the rage.

None of the early contenders could quite match the fascinating rhythm of "rest, residue, and remainder," which had become common by the late eighteenth century. Along the way the law—and the English language—lost some marvelous synonyms, like the fifteenth-century term **overplus**.

Rest, residue, and remainder has been described as a "ritual utterance"—a sort of incantation that lawyers hope will bring good luck. There is no particular technical significance to any of those words, although lawyers do occasionally take a stab at creating bogus pedigrees for them. In the eighteenth and nineteenth centuries, some courts followed the English case of *Hogan* v. *Jackson,* in which the court decided that "remainder" referred to real estate, while "residue" referred to personal property. By the early twentieth century, courts came to their senses and recognized the phrase for what it is: pure redundancy.

Even today, standard legal formbooks slavishly repeat the triple-R formula, although several of them conceded as long ago as the 1960s that the words are not necessary. Professor Crump also defends the use of "rest, residue, and remainder," which he calls "the tripartite approach," thus lending the phrase a degree of dignity that might safely be called overplus. The fact remains that one can use relatively plain expressions like "all other property" or "all property left over" without any trouble.

THE
PARTY
OF THE
FIRST
PART

158

THE DOWER JONES INDEX

Which brings us to the big question: Who gets the stuff? Whoever the testator wants—sort of. The law puts a few restrictions on your right to give away your loot. The most important limitation, historically, is that married people generally must leave something to their surviving spouses. The rules in this area go by the traditional names of **dower** and **curtesy**.

"Dower," which is related to endow, refers to the common law right of a widow to a certain share, usually one-third, of her late husband's estate. Technically, a man was said to "endow" his wife with this property right as part of the marriage ceremony. This concept took root early in America, making its first appearance in the 1648 Laws and Liberties of Massachusetts.

A widow who holds some of her late husband's property by virtue of dower is known as a **dowager**, although the word seems naked unless joined with an aristocratic title (the Dowager Countess). The word "dower" is also related to **dowry**, the money or property that a wife brings to a marriage.

Curtesy (an archaic spelling of courtesy) was a widower's right to a life tenancy in his late wife's lands. The only glitch was that in the old days a woman—though she might inherit and own property—had no power to convey it. So the grieving husband was said to receive his life tenancy "by the curtesy of England." And England was courteous indeed—to a fault, one might say—since a widower got 100 percent of his late wife's lands, while a widow got only a third of her late husband's wealth.

All this mumbo jumbo was made necessary in part by the legal doctrine of the **unity of marriage**. This is not the romantic notion that "two flesh become one." Rather, as a legal matter, husband and wife literally become one person, namely, the husband. As Blackstone put it,

> the very being or legal existence of a woman is suspended during the marriage, or is at least incorporated and consolidated into that of the husband.

In 1873, the Illinois Supreme Court approvingly cited the maxim "that a woman had no legal existence separate from her husband." This is why when a wife killed her husband, it was considered not merely murder, but the distinct crime of **petit treason**. In any event, since she had no independent legal existence, the wife could not bequeath property without special rules.

Dower and curtesy were critical to planning the dynastic marriages of great families. Indeed, marriage and estates—matrimony and patrimony, if you will—have always been closely related concepts in the law. In England, until 1970, divorce and probate matters were heard by the same court, which, oddly enough, also heard cases involving shipping disasters. The reason for combining these courts was that they all supposedly operated on principles of Roman law. To the lawyers who practiced there, the Divorce, Probate, and Admiralty Court was commonly referred to as the court of **Wills, Wives, and Wrecks**.

Nowadays, dower and curtesy have been abolished in England. In some American states, these old terms have been replaced by the scintillatingly modern **statutory share**. In other states, dower and curtesy remain on the books, but the distinction between them has been obliterated. It all amounts to the same thing: The surviving spouse is entitled to a set share of the deceased spouse's estate.

One can leave property to one's children (sometimes pretentiously referred to as **issue**), but one is not obliged to. A relatively recent development in the law allows children to inherit whether born in or out of wedlock. Historically, the law prohibited bequests to **bastards**, a term that derives from the Old French *fils de bast,* literally a "packsaddle child," in contrast to one conceived in the marriage bed. Although the legal bias against them has changed,

THE
PARTY
OF THE
FIRST
PART

160

bastard remains a standard legal term, found in every legal dictionary. As is **bastardy**, which can mean either the act of begetting a bastard or the state of being one.

In an effort to reform legal language, it became fashionable for many years to use the term **illegitimate** instead of bastard. More recently, lawyers have begun to realize that "illegitimate" isn't really much nicer. Lawyers now tend toward the literal, if cumbersome, **child born out of wedlock**. For those in search of a pithy phrase, there are traditional Latin terms that are sure to make an impression. In the ancient common law, children born out of wedlock were known variously as:

Son of nobody—*filius nullius*;
Son of the people—*filius populi*; or
Bastard brother—*frater nutricius* (and delicious?)

Not only were "bastards" excluded from one's estate, but so also were severely deformed children. These unfortunate offspring were called, with all the sensitivity that the law could summon, **monsters**—a term that appeared in law dictionaries as recently as 1922. The theory, as the lawyer Henry Swinburne summarized in his *Brief Treatise on Testaments and Last Wills* (1590), was that "the law doth not presume that Creature to have the Soul of a Man, which hath a Form and Shape so strange and different from the Shape of a Man."

The best that can be said about this dark corner of the law is that it was evidently not easy to qualify as a monster. According to Swinburne, a monster must have a human body but "a head like unto a Dog's Head, or to the

Head of an Ass, or a Raven, or Duck [*now come on*], or of some other Beast or Bird." Although the monster doctrine appears to have been abandoned in all courts, it would still be wise to consult a lawyer if you plan to leave your fortune to, say, a minotaur.

FERTILE OCTOGENARIANS AND THE MEN WHO LOVE THEM

THE
PARTY
OF THE
FIRST
PART

162

Law students and people with dynastic ambitions invariably run into a seventeenth-century doctrine called the **Rule Against Perpetuities**. This rule prevents you from leaving your house to your eldest son, and then to *his* eldest son, and so on, forever. The problem with that sort of gift-that-keeps-on-giving is that the title to your house remains **contingent** indefinitely, meaning that each generation is obliged to pass it on to the next. The Rule Against Perpetuities arose to ensure that title to property will **vest** absolutely at some definite point, so that the heirs will be free to sell it.

According to the Rule, you may not leave property in limbo for longer than the **perpetuities period**, an amount of time that is measured by the lifetime of a real person identified in your will (referred to as a **life in being**) plus twenty-one years. If you leave your house to your son Fred for the duration of his life, and then to Fred's yet-unborn eldest child, that bequest is within the perpetuities period. Fred is a life in being, and title to the house will vest in the grandchildren immediately after Fred's life is over. If you want, you can even make your grandchildren wait for twenty-one years after Fred's death before they get absolute title to the house; but that's as far as the law allows.

When a will is challenged for violating the Rule Against Perpetuities, it won't do any good to show that the bequest will *probably* vest within the perpetuities period—"probably" doesn't cut it. The court will strike down the bequest if it can imagine any scenario in which the testator's property will remain contingent for too long.

The law's fastidious approach to perpetuities has led to some strange twists on legal language. One way to extend the life of a bequest is to measure it by a life in being who has nothing to do with the testator, but who might be expected to enjoy longevity. For a time, it was popular among wealthy Englishmen to leave property tied up in family trusts "until 21 years after the death of the last of Queen Victoria's grandchildren." An American version, known as the **Kennedy Clause**, began to appear in the 1970s in commercial trusts (like wills, trusts are subject to the Rule Against Perpetuities). The Kennedy Clause typically reads as follows:

> In no event shall the trust continue beyond the expiration of 21 years from the death of the last survivor of the descendants of Joseph P. Kennedy, Sr., the late Ambassador to the Court of St. James.

According to a 2005 CBS News report, more than six thousand publicly filed legal documents in the United States contain a Kennedy Clause.

Bequests that are not saved by a Kennedy Clause may be ruined by the **Fertile Octogenarian**—an imaginary creature who represents the legal assumption that every person, regardless of age, is capable of procreation. The Fertile Octogenarian creates mischief in a number of ways. For example, let's say that Mr. Jones leaves property,

> "to my Aunt Polly for her life, and then to Aunt Polly's grandchildren."

At the time of Mr. Jones's death (which is when the will takes effect), Aunt Polly is eighty-five years old, with several children but no grandchildren. The bequest would be invalid because, under the **Fertile Octogenarian Rule**, Aunt Polly might still have another child. That child, who is not yet a life in being, might give birth to Aunt Polly's grandchild more than twenty-one years after Aunt Polly's death.

Incidentally, the law also assumes that children under five are as fruitful as old Aunt Polly. This principle was long ago dubbed the **Precocious Toddler Rule**. Alongside the Fertile Octogenarian and the Precocious Toddler— rounding out the law's hypothetical freak show—is the **Unborn Widow**. The Unborn Widow will be trotted out when, for example, Mr. Smith leaves property to his married son John for life, and then,

> "to John's widow for her life, and then to John's surviving children."

One might think that the word "widow" refers to John's current wife, and that is presumably what Mr. Smith meant. But if the will is challenged, courts will test its validity by assuming that "widow" refers to a person not yet born.

THE
PARTY
OF THE
FIRST
PART

164

Via the **Unborn Widow Rule**, the law rather rudely asserts not only that John's widow will be somebody other than his current wife, but that she will be a much younger woman. Now we have a problem because Mr. Smith's bequest will potentially tie up property for the entirety of his son's life, plus that of John's putative widow, who is not yet a life in being and might live more than twenty-one years after John's death.

It is slightly unnerving to know that if your will ever ends up in probate court, the fate of your hard-earned property may depend on a judge's determination of how your bequests would operate among a cast of fictional characters. But then, there probably isn't one judge in a thousand who will claim to have any insight into the testator's actual intentions. What are they anyway—psychics?

Judges take a certain malicious delight in reminding people of this, claiming that all they can do is interpret the words before them. And the way they go about it is by using standard rules of interpretation, also known as **canons of construction**—"construction" in the sense that the court must "construe" the will. The Fertile Octogenarian and her sprightly friends are products of the canons of construction.

Lawyers are trained to write wills that make sense according to the canons of construction, even if those wills are indecipherable to their clients. Recall Professor Crump's point that a will is not the sort of document that is routinely read "by someone who needs to understand it"—apparently clients do not "need" to understand their own wills. And so, every day, nonlawyers are told that they must pay huge sums for vitally important documents that might as well be written in a foreign tongue.

Is it time for a revolution? In 2000, an Englishman named John Middleton asked a local law firm to write a will that would leave his money to two trusts. In due course he received a document of such bewildering complexity as to make a dyed-in-the-wool Precision lawyer blush. Here is one paragraph (quoted, not admiringly, in the Plain English Campaign's newsletter):

THE
PARTY
OF THE
FIRST
PART

166

> ANY Executor for the time being hereof being a Solicitor or other person engaged in a profession or business shall be entitled to charge retain and be paid in priority to all other bequests hereby made all usual professional or other charges for business done by him or his firm in relation to proving this my Will and obtaining Probate thereof and in the execution or otherwise in relation to the trusts hereof and also his reasonable charges in addition to disbursements for other work and business done and all time spent by him or his firm in connection with matter arising in the premises including matters which might or should have been attended to in person by a trustee not being a Solicitor and any Executor shall be entitled to retain any brokerage or other commission which may be received personally or by such Executor's firm in respect of any transaction carried out in the administration of my Estate and the trusts thereof for which the Executor or his firm is in the normal course of business allowed or paid brokerage or other commission notwithstanding that the receipt of such brokerage or commission was produced by an exercise by such Executor of powers vested in him hereby or by law

Which is a 211-word way of saying that an executor can perform professional services for the estate and charge the estate for those services. For that paragraph and fourteen more pages of the same, Middleton was charged £300. There was no punctuation in the document. Punctuation, evidently, cost extra.

Middleton refused to pay. "If I buy a product from a shop or a service from a provider," he wrote to the law firm, "I expect to have a product or service that is fit for the purpose for which it is bought. The wills produced by [you] were not fit for the purpose since neither I nor my wife could understand them." He threatened to report the firm to a legal disciplinary committee, and the firm withdrew its bill.

Another man who struck a blow for plain English wills was Jack Kelly, the father of Grace Kelly and a successful businessman in his own right. Although he had more than enough money to pay lawyers to write his will, he did it himself. Kelly's will (reproduced in Robert Menchin's 1966 book, *The Last Caprice*) begins:

> I will attempt to write my own will in the hope that it will be understandable and legal. Kids will be called "kids" and not "issue" and it will not be cluttered up with "parties of the first part," "per stirpes," "perpetuities," "quasi-judicial," "to wit," and a lot of other terms that I am sure are only used to confuse those for whose benefit it is written.

DON'T TRY THIS AT HOME

It looks so simple, but don't be deceived. People like John Middleton and Jack Kelly are unusually brave. Most people, even self-made successes, rarely have the courage to face off against a platoon of lawyers eager to load up a will with technical jargon. When confronted by bequests, remainders, codicils, and the like, the average person tends to stare into the middle distance muttering "Rosebud."

You yourself might be feeling sufficiently confident at this point to march into your lawyer's office and demand a plain English will. "None of this excess verbiage, you hear?"

"No problem," says the lawyer. And then, with a hint of a smile, he adds: "Just one question: Would you like to bequeath your property *per stirpes*?"

You will no doubt begin to fidget as your mind races to figure out what your lawyer means by *per stirpes:* Strips? Stripes? Stirrups?

Rosebud?

Pull yourself together. *Per stirpes* is a Latin term meaning "by the branches" or "by the stocks." It is meant to describe the testator's intention to distribute property equally among various "branches" of a family. If, for example, you leave money to your three siblings *per stirpes,* and if one of them dies before you (or, as the law clinically puts it, **predeceases** you), then that sibling's share gets divided among his children, rather than being allocated to the surviving siblings.

One way to avoid using obscure Latin phrases would be to explain all of this in English. It would take more words than *per stirpes,* but then, plain language does not always mean maximum brevity; it means maximum clarity. Professor Crump, incidentally, states that substituting an English phrase for *per stirpes* "may be inadvisable."

The technical jargon that clutters up most wills is not "legal" in the sense that it is required by any law. Lawyers

THE
PARTY
OF THE
FIRST
PART

168

use this language out of tradition and a misguided sense of caution. The good news is that, in most wills, the intention is so straightforward that not even legalese can conceal it: the testator just wants all of his or her money to go to the next of kin.

The bad news is that the courts are not absolutely certain what the word "money" means. But that is the subject of the next chapter.

8

THE ROOT OF ALL EVIL

Choate: *That which has become perfected or ripened as e.g. a choate lien.*

— *BLACK'S LAW DICTIONARY*

Choate: *An erroneous word, framed to mean "finished," "complete," as if the in- of inchoate were the Latin negative.*

— *OXFORD ENGLISH DICTIONARY*

As she lay on her deathbed, Nellie Hodgson, a spinster, knew the end was drawing near. Her worldly possessions were kept in an attaché case next to her bed: She had £800 in cash and £600 in savings certificates, not a trivial sum at the time—1934.

She quickly wrote a will. She had been a children's nurse before taking ill and she sentimentally left all of her **"money"** to two of her charges: John Derek Fortescu Flannery and John Douglas Stewart Nowell.

After Hodgson's death, Flannery and Nowell were surprised to discover that instead of sharing £1,400, they would get only the £800 cash. The British government had seized the £600 worth of savings certificates as "ownerless goods," or *bona vacantia*, as the law sometimes calls it.

The government's reasoning was that when Hodgson used the word "money" in her will, she must have been referring only to the cash. Despite the absurdity of the proposition—that Hodgson had purposely let the £600 of certificates go ownerless—the courts sided with the government.

"Revolting to common sense," was how one British commentator reacted to the Hodgson case—but he also conceded that the judge's reasoning was "not uncommon" among the courts. For centuries, the law has had very particular definitions of the word "money," ones that are usually at odds with those used by the average person.

The 1991 edition of *Black's Law Dictionary* states that "money" in "usual and ordinary acceptation" means "coins and paper currency." And yet, one doubts that many people would actually acceptate that definition. It's not the way people talk. When you ask "Where does her money come from?" you don't mean "Where did she get those coins?" When an armed robber demands "your money or your life," you'd be well advised not to quibble about whether your Rolex technically constitutes "money."

Nowhere has the law's blinkered approach to money had a more drastic effect than in the field of wills—as the Hodgson case shows. It all began with a 1725 decision of an English court that established what was known as "money in the strict sense," that is, the doctrine that the word "money" when used in a will refers only to cash on hand and cash in a demand deposit account.

As we saw in Chapter 7, courts have a long tradition of disregarding the commonsense meaning of a will when it conflicts with the established rules of interpretation known as canons of construction. Money in the strict sense was one of the most powerful canons ever—a regular howitzer. (Thank you, and don't forget to tip your waitress.)

There are no reliable statistics, but it is likely that thousands of unfortunate souls were disinherited because somebody was careless enough to bequeath them "money" rather than "all my property real and personal" or some such legal piffle. The judges, of course, were well aware of what they were doing. With an almost comical regularity, judges in probate cases offered abject apologies when their strict interpretation of money led to perverse results. To take three examples from the last century:

> "It is painful to be obliged to come to the conclusion to which I have come";
> "I wish very much that I could accede to the argument of [counsel], because I cannot resist the

impression that [that is what] this testatrix intended"; and

"the conclusion at which I have arrived is one to which I confess I come with some little regret."

The English courts finally abolished the "strict sense" of money in 1942. It was in a case involving yet another spinster, this one named Emily Morgan, in which the traditional interpretation of money would have excluded £32,000 (out of a total estate of £33,000) from the operation of Ms. Morgan's will. An appellate court decided that that was taking things just a little too far.

THE
PARTY
OF THE
FIRST
PART

174

In throwing out the "strict sense" of money, the appellate court was expressly trying to prevent another Hodgson case. "In the future," said the Court, "the resources of the Crown will receive no such flagitious increment." *Flagitious,* in case you were wondering, means wicked or heinous.

Well into the twentieth century, most American courts followed the British canon of construction regarding money in the strict sense. In fact, the doctrine still lurks in the background of some American court decisions. In 1991, the Texas Court of Appeals held that references to "money" in a will meant cash on hand and on deposit, but did not include other assets like stocks and bonds.

CENTS AND SENSIBILITY

Although judges insisted for two hundred years that the word "money" meant cash, they never quite decided what **cash** meant. A textbook on drafting wills warns that the meaning of the word "cash" is so uncertain that it "has resulted in litigation." And those who assume that the legal definition of cash must, at a minimum, be more precise than that of "money" can be forgiven for pounding their heads against the wall when they discover that *Black's Law Dictionary* defines cash as "money or the equivalent."

Back in Plain English land, cash really means "coins or bills" (*Oxford Desk Dictionary*). Not Monopoly bills, but the official stuff. The law books refer to this as **legal tender**. Legal tender is that which a creditor is required to accept when "tendered" in payment of a debt. "Tender" comes from the French *tendre* (to hold out), which also gives rise to the use of tender as an adjective and even occasionally as an adverb, as when Elvis sang "love me tender."

Money is a broader concept; it includes legal tender, but also anything that passes as a "medium of exchange," as one federal court put it. The flexibility of the term "money" has allowed lawyers to come up with dozens of different, and at times contradictory, definitions. While probate courts were busy narrowing the definition of money, criminal prosecutors were doing their best to expand it. This is because all sorts of criminal laws prohibit things done with, or in exchange for, money.

In Texas, for example, a court once decided that a bottle of beer could count as money. That's because a criminal statute prohibited the playing of pool if "money" were bet on the game. Small wonder, perhaps, that Texans like to put their money where their mouth is.

In San Diego, a zealous district attorney in the 1940s argued that a free pinball game constituted money. That definition would have allowed him to seize pinball machines as illicit gambling devices since they offer "money" as a prize. But the appellate court rejected the argument, declaring flatly—and quite philosophically—that money does not equal "amusement," even in the form of a complimentary pinball game.

There have even been cases in which men's lives depended on the legal definition of money. In 1777, an accountant named Harrison was caught altering an account entry for banknotes (paper currency issued by private banks). He was brought to trial in London for "forging a receipt for money"—a crime that was then punishable by death. Harrison successfully argued that the law did not apply to him because his forgery did not involve "money," but only banknotes, which were not legal tender. At the time, only gold and silver coin counted as legal tender. Harrison's case proved to be a convenient precedent for soft-hearted judges who were reluctant to send men to the gallows for cooking the books.

Eventually, accounting fraud ceased to be a capital offense—all good things must end—and so the rule in Harrison's case quietly vanished from criminal law. In the meantime, however, the rule had infiltrated commercial law, where the courts began to rigidly define "money" in commercial contracts as legal tender. That created immense problems for Americans involved in international business. An exporter, for example, might hold a promissory note to be paid, say, in French francs. An American court of the 1950s may not have enforced such a note because it was not a promise to pay "money." Nowadays, the Uniform Commercial Code (which exists in all 50 states) specifies that the word "money" in commercial contracts includes foreign currency.

THE
PARTY
OF THE
FIRST
PART

176

The definition of **dollar** is a persistently controversial subject among many Americans. To illustrate the issue—and at the risk of alarming you—I have to point out that the dollar bills in your wallet are not themselves dollars. Not exactly, anyway.

A **dollar** is a measure of value, the basic unit of American currency which has been prescribed by a law even older than the Constitution. Congress adopted the dollar in 1785, setting its initial value at 375 64/100 grains of fine silver. A **dollar bill**, on the other hand, is the common name for a **Federal Reserve Note** (that's what it says right at the top of the bill), which is a written promise by the Fed to pay a dollar's worth of something at some later date.

At one point in time that something would have been gold or silver. For much of America's history, the only things that counted as official "dollars" were gold and silver coins, known as **specie**. Then there was paper money, but scrupulously redeemable in gold under the **Gold Standard Act of 1900**. Today, if you take your Federal Reserve Note to the Fed and ask for a real "dollar," all you'll get— aside from a funny look—is a newer, crisper dollar bill. The reason for this is that in 1971 the Nixon Administration took the United States off the gold standard, leaving the country with Federal Reserve Notes that are legal tender but have no intrinsic value.

The majority of people who pause to consider this state of affairs simply shrug their shoulders and go back to whatever it was they were doing. Nonetheless, the notion that paper dollars are illegal—indeed, unconstitutional—is

THE
ROOT
OF ALL
EVIL

177

deeply held by thousands of Americans, most of whom also happen to believe that the federal government is secretly implanting microchips in their brains.

In 1980, a Kansas man named Gary Rickman got in trouble with the IRS for declaring that he had no income whatsoever, despite the fact that he had admittedly been employed as a mathematics instructor at a community college. At his trial, Rickman explained that his income was zero "dollars," because all he had earned were measly Federal Reserve Notes. For the purposes of tax law, Rickman contended, one's earnings must be valued in good old-fashioned specie—gold dollars.

Rickman bolstered his argument by pointing out that the Form 1040 uses the dollar sign ($), which, as everyone knows, is a symbol that refers exclusively to coins, not notes. The idea, it seems, is that the dollar sign comes from the old Spanish Dollar, or piece of eight, which was a silver coin at the time that the "dollar" was adopted as the unit of American currency. The federal court of appeals referred to this theory as "the height of absurdity" (but they would, they're part of the conspiracy) and upheld his conviction. Contrary to Rickman's argument, nobody is certain what the dollar sign stands for; it could be "Spanish Dollar," but various experts have held that it is a monogram for peso, piaster, potosi, schilling, or even slave.

Counterfeiters, oddly enough, also tend to be purists about the meaning of the word "dollar." In 1975, John Grismore was arrested in Utah for "uttering and dealing in counterfeit obligations of the United States"—**uttering** being the technical term for putting bogus money into circulation. In Grismore's case, he didn't so much *utter* counterfeit notes as shout them at the top of his lungs. Federal

THE
PARTY
OF THE
FIRST
PART

178

agents found him with over $650,000 in counterfeit bills. In his defense, Grismore gamely asserted that he had merely copied Federal Reserve Notes rather than dollars. Mr. Grismore, one imagines, became the toast of the prison law library. He had eight years to peruse the collection.

The claims made by Rickman, Grismore, and hundreds of other litigants who have followed in their futile footsteps are not completely without foundation. The Constitution gives Congress only the power "to coin money," which, in the eighteenth century, would have been taken quite literally: minting, not printing. Nothing in the Constitution explicitly allows the federal government to print money.

What's more, Article I of the Constitution prohibits any state from "mak[ing] anything but gold or silver coin a tender in the payment of debts." Certainly, a good argument can be made that the Constitution sought to banish paper money, especially since the paper Continental Dollars had been a disaster under the Articles of Confederation.

The problem is that these arguments were long ago rejected by Congress and the Supreme Court. It was in 1862, faced with the enormous cost of the Civil War, that Congress passed the **Legal Tender Act**, which authorized the government to issue paper notes that were declared legal tender but that could not be exchanged for specie. The notes were printed in green ink and popularly referred to as "greenbacks."

Various lawsuits challenging the legality of greenbacks clogged up the courts for years. In the 1884 **Legal Tender Case**, the Supreme Court held that the federal government could issue paper money, whether or not it was backed by specie. The Court has never shown the slightest inclination to reconsider the matter. Although, as we saw, the United States did return to the gold standard in 1900, the Legal Tender Case provided the constitutional basis for the government's 1971 decision to give it up.

Currency protestors still don't believe it. Some have even taken to using alternative currencies such as the privately minted silver "Liberty Dollar." They insist that precious metal coins harken back to the simpler era of specie when "a dollar was a dollar." As far as legal language goes, that argument is, well, specious. Hard currency actually makes it considerably more difficult to define a "dollar" because the value of metal coins can easily fall out of sync with their face value.

THE
PARTY
OF THE
FIRST
PART

180

In 1981, a federal appellate court held, essentially, that $1 sometimes means $5. A lawyer named Gary Joslin billed his client $200 for services, but specified that the fee was to be paid in silver dollars. The IRS estimated his income from that transaction to be $1,000—despite the fact that silver dollars have a face value of $1 and, if brought to the Treasury, would be redeemed by a $1 Federal Reserve Note. The reason is that the **numismatic value**—the silver content, plus the value of the coin as a collectible—of a silver dollar at the time was about $5.

The word "dollar" is not even the exclusive legal name for American money. The United States Code says "The money of account of the United States shall be expressed in *dollars or units*" (emphasis mine). Why, one wonders, has the "unit" not permeated the popular culture? Optimistic types could leap out of bed feeling like a million units; philosophers could decry the cult of the almighty unit; and desperadoes could draw their six-shooters for a fistful of units.

Sadly, the potential hilarity of currency talk generally goes unnoticed. The next time you find yourself at a department store cash register, put on an apologetic face and start the following conversation:

"I'm sorry, all I seem to have in my wallet are Federal Reserve Notes. Do you take those?"

"Well, I don't—"

"Oh, and I don't have anything smaller than a fifty-unit note. Can you make change for a fifty-unit Federal Reserve Note?"

PLAYING THE MARKET

No discussion of money would be complete without mentioning **stocks** and **bonds**. In the Emily Morgan case—the one that overturned the flagitious Hodgson case—the court ruled that the statement " 'I have my money invested . . . in stocks and shares' is not an illegitimate use of the word 'money.' " Nor is it unusual, since millions of people say words to that effect every day. Stocks and bonds have become the great vessels of wealth in today's world.

The law uses the word **security** (from Latin *securus,* "without care") as an umbrella term for stocks, bonds, and similar investments. A security is an investment in an enterprise, in the form of either an ownership interest, or a right to share in profits, or a loan to the enterprise.

A **stock** represents an ownership interest in a company. If, say, your uncle gives you a few shares of Microsoft stock, then you own a small (*very* small) percentage of Microsoft's assets. The word comes from the Old English *stocc,* meaning "tree trunk." At some point around the fifteenth century, the word came to represent a money box or sum of money, perhaps because money, like a tree trunk, is a foundation for future growth.

In the early 1600s the word was borrowed for a new form of commercial endeavor, the **joint stock company**. Many of the first joint stock companies were formed to settle the New World. Thus, in 1607, an Englishman named Richard Hakluyt proposed

THE
PARTY
OF THE
FIRST
PART

182

the raising of a PUBLIC STOCK to be employed for the peopling and discovering of such countries as may be found most convenient for the supply of those defects which this Realm of England most requires.

That may have been the first **IPO** (Initial Public Offering) in history. Notwithstanding all the excitement, Queen Elizabeth declined to invest.

A **bond** is an **IOU** from a corporation or government—when you buy one, you are lending money to that entity. The word (from the Middle English *band*) is related to such terms as "bind" and "bound," as seen in such everyday expressions as "my word is my bond."

There is a vast body of securities laws, most of which were enacted in the wake of the stock market crash of 1929. The basic thrust of these laws can be summed up in a single word: **disclosure**. You can sell an almost infinite variety of investments; however, if you don't tell the investing public exactly what they're getting themselves into, you'll be subject to private lawsuits and even criminal prosecution.

But only if what you're selling is, in fact, a security. Any number of crafty entrepreneurs have tried to avoid liability under the securities laws by claiming that the particular investment that they were hawking falls outside the definition of a security. These arguments usually fail. In various cases over the years, state and federal courts have held that all of the following things fit within the definition of a "security":

- Earthworms
- Scotch whisky
- Cosmetics
- Muskrats
- Beavers
- Chinchillas
- Cemetery lots
- Cattle embryos
- Fruit trees

To be clear, this does not mean that the next time you order a glass of Scotch you can congratulate yourself on making a wise investment. What distinguishes a security—as the courts decided in these cases—is that the investor hopes to profit entirely from the efforts of other people. So if you purchase a barrel of Scotch with the intention of bottling and selling it (or drinking it) yourself, it isn't a security. But if somebody sells you the same barrel with the promise that *he* will market the stuff and share the profits with you, then it's a security just as much as a share of stock.

So, for those looking to make a killing in the Scotch, or chinchilla, market, you have the right to full disclosure from the person offering the investment. Disclosure usually arrives via a document called a **prospectus** (Latin for "a view"), which, depending on the context, might also be called a **private placement memorandum** or **offering memorandum**.

Traditionally, prospectuses consisted of great swaths of intricate boilerplate (see Chapter 2) that took hours to slog through. Part of the problem was what one law firm dubbed the **Three Times Rule,** which stands for "put everything in three times." The idea is that if an investor claims to have been duped, the company's lawyers can say "Your Honor, we disclosed that information three times!"

America's most successful investor, Warren Buffett, wrote that in his many decades of reading prospectuses, "Too often, I've been unable to decipher just what is being said or, worse yet, had to conclude that nothing is being said."

In the mid-1990s, the Securities and Exchange Commission gave the legal profession a failing grade, disclosurewise, finding that "the technical and dense legalese of current disclosure documents hides the information that is necessary for investors to make informed investment decisions."

By 1997, the SEC had identified a particular need for plain English in three distinct parts of the prospectus: the beginning, middle, and end. Actually, it was the cover page, summary statement, and discussion of risk factors. The SEC issued a proposed rule that would require "plain English" in those three sections, and "clear and concise" language in the rest of the prospectus—thus creating a somewhat un-plain distinction, but we'll overlook that.

THE
PARTY
OF THE
FIRST
PART

184

The SEC was clearly on the right track. The proposed rule contained six basic principles of plain English:

1. active voice
2. short sentences
3. definite, concrete, everyday words
4. use of tables or bullet points for complex material
5. no legal jargon or highly technical business terms
6. no multiple negatives

One might think that these are uncontroversial—indeed, unimpeachable—guidelines for clear legal writing. Predictably, lawyers objected.

The American Bar Association protested, in a letter to the SEC, that the plain-English rule would lead to documents lacking in **material information** (that is, *important* information). This is nothing more than the old Precision School canard that plainly written documents are necessarily less precise. Of course, the ABA did not try to explain the value of any information, even "material" information, that is written in language that nobody can understand.

The SEC wisely brushed aside the ABA's objection and went ahead with its rule. The agency has published a handbook on the use of plain English—which ought to be required reading for all lawyers—including some dramatic before-and-after comparisons.

To take one example, the SEC quotes a prospectus describing certain "notes" issued by MBNA Bank. In the original document, the cover page states, in language apparently designed to encourage a man contemplating suicide to just get on with it:

Each certificate will represent an undivided interest in the Trust and the interest of the Certificateholders of each class or Series will include the right
to receive a varying percentage of each month's collections with respect to the Receivables of the Trust
at the times, in the manner and to the extent described herein and, with respect to any Series offered
hereby, in the Related Prospectus Supplement.

When all that gobbledygook is boiled down according to
plain-language principles, you end up with:

The Certificateholders will receive interest and
principal payments from a varying percentage of
credit card account collections.

186 Granted, it's still not exactly beach reading, but at least it
makes sense—nothing more complicated than "principal"
and "interest," and if you don't understand those words,
perhaps better not to invest.

Not that the plain-English rules solve all of the ills of
prospectuses. Repetition is still a problem. The law firm
that coined the term "Three Times Rule" now advises its
clients "to still say it three times, but say it in plain English." Ho hum.

Despite the naysayers, the rule *has* changed the behavior of public companies—no doubt partly because the SEC
has threatened to do spot checks of company filings to ensure compliance with plain-English principles. When
companies run afoul of the rules, the SEC can substantially
delay their access to the financial markets. Considering
that for some companies a delay in raising capital can be

fatal, the SEC's powers are truly extraordinary. Who would have imagined that a federal agency would have the authority to punish large corporations for using bad English? The mind reels as we cut to a large office complex in New York City:

> **Secretary:** Mr. Smithers, it's the FBI here to see you.
>
> **Smithers:** Tell them I'm busy—oh, hello, Officer. Nice day, isn't it?
>
> **FBI Agent:** Cut the small talk. I've read your latest prospectus. What made you think you could get away with all those run-on sentences? Huh? Huh? What kind of a twisted mind would lump all of those subordinate clauses together?
>
> **Smithers:** But I didn't want to miss any material information!
>
> **FBI Agent:** Save your Precision School clichés for the judge, Mister, I'm taking you in.

The success of the plain-English rule left the ABA with egg on its face. In 1999, the organization fired back a tit-for-tat resolution urging federal agencies to use plain language in *their* documents. Touché, indeed.

THAT'S WHY THE LADY IS A TRAMP, YOUR HONOR

The absence of money gives rise to almost as many legal terms as money itself. The word **bankrupt** comes from the Italian expression *banca rotta,* which means "broken bench." The first bankers were Italian money changers who worked at benches known as *bancas*. According to legend, the term *banca rotta* comes from the fact that insolvent money changers had their benches literally broken to pieces. Alternatively, the *rotta* could just be a metaphor for "ruined," in the same way that we use "broke" in English to describe a penniless person.

Although *banca rotta* described a condition, legal English originally used "bankrupt" to refer to a person. A merchant who could not meet his obligations was "adjudged a bankrupt." Nowadays, federal law uses **bankrupt** as an adjective to describe the state of being *banca rotta*. The bankrupt person, under federal law, is known as a **debtor**—although that term is also used in a general sense to refer to anyone who owes money to a **creditor**.

Britain and the United States developed a complex system of laws to deal with the poor. Until the nineteenth century, these were called, with an admirable directness, **Poor Laws**. To a large extent, the Poor Laws were aimed at punishing poor people. Although an ancient legal maxim has it that "**the law is safest for the poor**," legions of poor men throughout history would beg, as it were, to differ.

The law traditionally assumed that any able-bodied beggar must have chosen to beg. Such people were branded as criminals, specifically as **sturdy beggars**, **sturdy vagabonds**, or **rogues**. These were all technical legal terms. Cowell's dictionary, for example, lists the offenses of being a "Roag [rogue] of the first degree" and "Roag of the second degree." The punishment for repeat roguery was death.

Before you laugh this off as a relic of history, you might take a glance at the official website of the Massachusetts legislature. It is still a crime in the Bay State to be a **vagrant** or a **vagabond**—the former being a beggar, the latter a

THE
PARTY
OF THE
FIRST
PART

188

person who is "known to be a pickpocket" and is caught acting "in a suspicious manner."

For those who don't fit into either category, Massachusetts has a separate offense of being a **tramp**. The criminal code provides that "an act of begging or soliciting **alms** [charity] . . . shall be prima facie evidence that such person is a tramp." To which, we might add, so is carrying one's possessions in a bundle tied to the end of stick and wearing a crumpled porkpie hat.

It seems unlikely that these Massachusetts laws would survive a court challenge today. Ever since the Supreme Court's 1972 decision in *Papachristou* v. *City of Jacksonville* (1972) the validity of all state vagrancy statutes has been in serious doubt. In the Papachristou case, the Court struck down a Florida law that explicitly targeted not only rogues and vagabonds, but also made it a crime to be an **habitual loafer**, a term that, sadly, went undefined.

In giving the court's opinion, Justice Douglas quotes Henry David Thoreau's essay in praise of **sauntering**, which, according to Thoreau, comes from the French *Sainte Terre* (Holy Land) because medieval vagabonds would beg for alms under the pretense of going to *la Sainte Terre*.

As a legal matter this was completely beside the point. Presumably Douglas was trying to show that, by striking down the Florida law, the Court was not unleashing hordes of "rogues," but only cheerful "saunterers." What you call things makes all the difference, as we'll see in the next chapter.

9

NAME THAT LAW

Peeping Tom statute: U.S. Criminal Law, an act outlawing intrusive voyeurism.

— *OXFORD ENGLISH DICTIONARY*

Vermont has no "Peeping Tom" statute.

— *TIMES ARGUS*, SEPTEMBER 26, 2004

In the summer of 2003, Congress was nearly unanimous in its desire to pass a law against unsolicited e-mail, otherwise known as spam. There was even consensus—with a few exceptions—about the appropriate content of an anti-spam statute. One of the only controversial aspects of the new law was what to call it. Some of the proposals included:

- **SPAM Act:** short for "Stop Pornography and Abusive Marketing Act"
- **RID Spam Act:** short for "Reduction in Distribution of Spam Act"
- **REDUCE Spam Act:** short for "Restrict and Eliminate the Delivery of Unsolicited Commercial Electronic Mail or Spam Act"

The winner was none of the above, but instead the even more tortured **CAN-SPAM Act**, which stands for "Controlling the Assault of Non-Solicited Pornography and Marketing Act." One can only imagine that small armies of congressional staffers pulled multiple all-nighters until the epiphany finally hit them:

> "We've been through this a hundred times. I'm telling you, it's not good enough to 'reduce' spam, we've got to can it!"
> "Can it? That's it, you nailed it: Can-Spam!"
> "Excellent! Double lattes on me."

Unfortunately, the whole effort backfired because critics of the law—who consider it ineffective—almost immediately dubbed it the "Yes, You Can Spam Act," turning what seemed to be a clever label into a political liability.

Congress devotes a surprising amount of time to coming up with names for laws. More time, it sometimes seems, than they spend actually thinking about the content of the laws. There's a reason for this: What you call a law can have a profound effect on the public's support for it. A law with a name like the **USA PATRIOT Act**, for example, is more likely to garner votes than the *Let's Subpoena Your Library Books Act*.

Speaking of which, statute names can be controversial—certainly, critics of the PATRIOT Act bristle at the suggestion that they are somehow *un*patriotic. In Maine, a 1996 law that created the first-in-the-nation program for public funding of elections was given the feel-good title of the **Maine Clean Elections Act**. Opponents of the law mounted a campaign to change the name—just the name, mind you—of the statute to the "Publicly Financed Elections Act." The opponents' goal was to make sure that people realized their tax dollars were going toward political commercials, just in case they wanted to demand better special effects, or anything like that.

A number of congressmen who voted against the 1996 **Defense of Marriage Act**, which exempts states from the obligation to recognize gay marriages from other states, singled out the title of the bill as one of their reasons for opposing it. In the House, one representative pointedly asked, "What are we defending marriage against?" The congressmen who tried to block the bill issued a committee report arguing "By far, the weakest part of the bill logically is its title."

The name of a law can even determine who makes it into the history books and who doesn't. The late Senator John Sherman, who served from 1881 to 1897, would almost certainly be forgotten today were it not for the fact that his name is attached to one of the most influential laws ever passed by Congress: the **Sherman Antitrust Act**. This was the first law to prohibit monopolies and other restraints on competition.

THE
PARTY
OF THE
FIRST
PART

194

Oddly enough, Senator Sherman did not write the law that bears his name. Rather, he had penned an earlier version that Congress rejected. The bill that did pass Congress was drafted by Senator George F. Hoar of Massachusetts. Out of deference to Sherman's early advocacy of antitrust, however, the law has lived on with his name while Senator Hoar has fallen into the deepest obscurity.

Taking credit for a law is not always a winning strategy. The National Prohibition Act—the one that outlawed booze—came to be known as the **Volstead Act** in honor of Andrew Volstead, a Republican representative from Minnesota who pushed the legislation through Congress. The Volstead Act was embodied in the Eighteenth Amendment, which was ratified in 1920. Two years later, Volstead was voted out of office. He retired to Minnesota, where, one imagines, he read about the rise and fall of Prohibition over steaming cups of Ovaltine.

BIRTH OF A LAW

Names like CAN-SPAM and Sherman Antitrust Act are known as **popular names**. A popular name is only one of several names that get attached to a law—it's the best known, but the least official of the statutory names.

When a law is newly enacted, it gets a **session number**—that is, a number that memorializes exactly when the law was passed in the life of a particular Congress, Parliament, or whatever. In Washington, session numbers begin with P.L., which stands for Public Law. A law called P.L. 102-89, for example, would be the eighty-ninth law passed by the 102nd Congress.

Next, a new law must receive a **code number**. That means somebody has to figure out where the law fits within the maze of existing laws, the **United States Code**. All federal laws are divided into fifty **titles**, which are further divided into subtopics and sections. The titles of the U.S. Code bear sturdy names like **Commerce**, **Labor**, and **Agriculture**. There is even a separate title for **Intoxicating Liquors**, thanks to Mr. Volstead and his colleagues.

It may be disquieting to learn that the responsibility for imposing order on federal legislation falls to obscure government lawyers in baggy polyester suits. But then, almost everything that government does is achieved by obscure people in baggy polyester suits. In fact, the legislative counsel who work for Congress are unsung heroes—taking what Congress gives them and making it fit, as logically as possible, into a coherent scheme of laws. Once codified, a law will be referred to like this:

15 U.S.C. §1

Translated, it means "Title 15 (Commerce) of the United States Code, Section One"—which happens, incidentally, to be the Sherman Act.

Most laws include a **long title**, also known as an **official title** or a **formal title**. In both the United States and Britain, the long title consists of the words "AN ACT to" followed by some very official-sounding words along the lines of

> AN ACT to reinstate the consolidated omnibus appropriation previously disaggregated from the Emergency Reauthorization of Administrative Services Act, and to prevent halitosis, and for other, further, and related purposes.

THE
PARTY
OF THE
FIRST
PART

196

There is venerable tradition of convoluted long titles. One of the best bad long titles comes from a British statute of 1750—it runs to nearly three hundred words. Admittedly, the title had a lot of ground to cover, as the statute dealt with a bewildering array of topics including coastal navigation, salmon fishing, court fees, and "the stealing or destroying of Turnips."

Long titles almost invariably fly in the face of plain English. Not only are they verbose, but they tend to combine language that is misleadingly vague—"AN ACT to make provision as regards contact with children" (they're talking about adoption)—with that which is needlessly technical—"to amend Part 10A of the Children Act 1989 in relation to Wales" (which conveys nothing to 99.9 percent of the population).

In 1992, the British organization Clarity issued a report urging Parliament to eliminate long titles altogether. "They give legislation an unhealthy look," the group wrote briskly—implying that laws should not only cast off their long titles, but also get some fresh air and wholesome exercise—"and serve no useful purpose that cannot be achieved in other ways." Unfortunately, Parliament ignored this recommendation and has continued to churn out statute after statute marred by the sickly pallor of long titles.

British politicians do, on occasion, attempt to make their long titles more reader friendly. Surfing through the minutes of the House of Lords, as one does, one discovers that the afternoon of April 19, 1999, was almost entirely devoted to a debate over the long title of a pollution control bill. The title began:

AN ACT to make provision for a new system of pollution prevention and control; and for related purposes. . . .

The blow-by-blow action was almost unbearably exciting. Lord Dixon-Smith and Lord Renton argued that the long title "tells us very little" and what it did say was inaccurate. Lord Dixon-Smith proposed an amendment to substitute a new long title, one that would "inform the public" as to the bill's true purpose. Lord Whitty, a government minister, said that he had received legal advice that the long title could not be altered, but he promised to seek further counsel on the matter. That prompted Baroness Hamwee to quip, "I hope that the Minister will be successful in obtaining advice that the Long Title should reflect what is in the Bill." By way of reply, Lord Dixon-Smith cryptically observed that "there are supposed to be more ways than one of killing a cat," and abruptly withdrew his amendment. And then they all went off to the Mad Hatter's Tea Party.

Session numbers, code numbers, and long titles all have one thing in common: They are of no use to a politician on the campaign trail. "Vote for Jones, proud sponsor of P.L. 102-89" just doesn't pack much of a punch. This is where popular names come in.

At first, popular names developed informally, by consensus of politicians, journalists, and assorted pundits. Nobody officially bestowed them. Beginning in the early twentieth century, Congress realized that they could expedite, and control, the process by inserting official **short titles** right into the text of statutes. The short titles were meant to be instantly "popular."

The use of short titles has been traced back as far as an agricultural bill of 1916 that had the audacity to call itself the **Federal Farm Loan Act**. Short titles, however, did not really take off until the New Deal, when a mass of complex legislation suddenly demanded some very clever packaging. This was the era of the **National Industrial Recovery Act**, the **Tennessee Valley Authority Act**, and the granddaddy of them all, the **Social Security Act**, a name that is considerably easier to remember than the long title:

> AN ACT to provide for the general welfare by establishing a system of Federal old-age benefits, and by enabling the several States to make more adequate provision for aged persons, blind persons, dependent and crippled children, maternal and child welfare, public health, and the administration of their unemployment compensation laws; to

THE
PARTY
OF THE
FIRST
PART

198

establish a Social Security Board; to raise revenue; and for other purposes.

For the most part, short titles represent an attempt to come up with a relatively catchy name for a new law. The key word here is *relatively,* since most of what Congress enacts is about as catchy as the **Watermelon Research and Promotion Act** (an actual statute). In such cases, the best Congress can do is to be straightforwardly descriptive, perhaps in the hope that no one will be bothered to pause long enough to think: research?

A certain enforced blandness is the general rule with legislation. Congress even manages to drain the excitement out of cars, trucks, and trains by their deft use of the phrase **Surface Transportation.** In Britain, when the government acted to crack down on marauding bands of soccer hooligans, Parliament reduced the whole unpleasantness of the subject into a single throat-clearing parenthetical: **The Football (Disorder) Act 2000.**

Whenever possible, lawmakers strive to give statutes names that people cannot disagree with, such as the **Clean Air Act,** the **Animal Welfare Act,** and the **Child Protection Act,** to name just a few. Who could be against those things? British parliamentarians employ the same technique, as can be seen in the unassailable **Equality Act 2004**—although one wonders what took them so long to get around to that one.

REAP WHAT YE SEED

Short titles often get even catchier when abbreviated to their initial letters, like NIRA for the National Industrial

Recovery Act. For those who care about such things—and that would be you if you've made it this far—abbreviations fall into two categories. An **acronym** is an abbreviation that forms a pronounceable word, even if the word has no independent meaning (NATO), while an **initialism** is one in which each letter is pronounced separately (IBM). Congress likes initialisms well enough, but it absolutely loves acronyms. Read any volume of federal law and the acronyms come tumbling off the page: NEPA, ERISA, RICO, DOMA, COBRA, FIFRA.

The holy grail of all this wordsmithery is an acronym that not only spells out real words, but words that relate to the statute: for instance, the CAN-SPAM Act. Linguists refer to acronyms like CAN-SPAM as **backronyms** because people compose them "backwards"; they start with the acronym and then try to string together a phrase with the appropriate initial letters. The most famous recent example of this was the USA PATRIOT Act, which stands for the "Uniting and Strengthening America by Providing Appropriate Tools Required to Intercept and Obstruct Terrorism Act."

A reference librarian at the University of Washington Law School named Mary Whisner actually took it upon herself to research the history of congressional backronyms, which she endearingly refers to as "cute acronyms." Whisner's findings, lucidly published in the *Law Library Journal,* show that Congress got into the cute-acronym game in 1988 with the **WARN Act** (the Worker Adjustment and Retraining Notification Act), which requires certain employers to give workers sixty days' advance notice before plant closings or major layoffs. Whisner identified 22 backronyms devised by Congress between 1988

THE
PARTY
OF THE
FIRST
PART

200

and 2003, including such buoyant titles as the **HOPE Act**, the **LIFT Act**, and the **SEED Act**, which, appropriately enough, was followed by the **REAP Act**. There is even a **CHIMP Act**, although it does not, unfortunately, address gorilla warfare.

Should you ever need to while away a rainy afternoon, try composing a good backronym. It's not that hard—even Congress can do it. The underlying phrase should be something rousing, and the resulting acronym instantly memorable. For example,

Reviving Efficiency and Employment by Leaving Entitlements alone and Cutting Taxes to Maintain the Economy for America and to Cut Taxes.

which, when properly abbreviated, becomes the RE-ELECT ME ACT. You may have noticed that cutting taxes appears twice in the title. That was just to give it an air of authenticity.

IT SEEMED LIKE A GOOD IDEA AT THE TIME

Despite the strenuous efforts of politicians to write laws that are, or at least sound, "popular," statute books are crammed full of titles that are astonishingly obscure. The **Non-Intercourse Act**, to take one example, has been federal law since 1790 and has, one would think, failed rather spectacularly in its stated purpose. It turns out that the title refers to intercourse in the sense of "commerce"; the law requires that any conveyance of Indian tribal lands be approved by the federal government. This was indeed a popular name in its day; so much so that in 1809 Congress passed another Non-Intercourse Act, this one aimed at trade with Britain and France. In the early nineteenth century, Americans were better off avoiding intercourse altogether (see Chapter 5).

Until 1938, British food merchants were subject to **An Acte for the well garblinge of spices**, which undoubtedly caused more than one grocer to scratch his head. *Garblinge* is a seventeenth-century word for "sifting." The method of presenting petitions to the British Parliament was dictated—until 1948—by the **Tumultuous Petitioning Act**. This statute did not actually require that petitions be accompanied by hordes of pitchfork-bearing peasants, but the name does give one a sense of how MPs regarded such popular supplications.

In 1988, the U.K. government issued the splendidly named **Zoonoses Order**, using a word so obscure that it does not even merit an entry in the *Oxford English Dictionary*. Unfortunately, the order itself fails to define, or even mention, that critical word anywhere other than the title. A medical dictionary—if one knows to look there— reveals that "zoonoses," also spelled "zoonosis," is any sort of disease that can be spread from animals to humans under natural conditions. The Zoonoses Order was originally intended to address salmonella. Yet, somehow, the word makes one think of aardvarks.

American state legislatures can always be relied upon to come up with obscure names for laws. One would be hard pressed, for example, to divine the contents of a statute known as the **Chuck E. Cheese Law**. In fact, this is the popular name for laws passed in Alabama, Arkansas, and Florida permitting arcade games—like those found in

THE
PARTY
OF THE
FIRST
PART

202

your classier pizza joints—to award coupons for prizes, an arrangement that would otherwise violate state gambling laws. Despite its jolly name, the law has proven to be controversial. In 2002, Alabama's Attorney General had his state's Chuck E. Cheese law ruled unconstitutional, meaning that the restaurants can no longer give out free coupons in that state. The unlimited refills policy, fortunately, has so far escaped constitutional challenge.

A casual glance at the Missouri legislature's Popular Name Table turns up such curiosities as the **Badman Fighting Act** and the **Seven Deadly Sins Act**. The former is a law prohibiting certain types of "extreme" fighting, evidently known as "badman fighting" or sometimes as "toughman fighting"—the Colorado version of the law is the **Toughman Fighting Act**. The latter defines seven serious felonies that require mandatory sentences, but the list of felonies does not actually correspond to the original seven sins. Sloth, for example, is still legal in Missouri— indeed, compulsory in some parts of the state.

Some laws are so narrowly focused that their popular names can never be truly popular. The **Adjustment to Lawful Resident Status of Certain Nationals of Countries for Which Extended Voluntary Departure Has Been Made Available Act** is duly listed in the Popular Names Table of the U.S. Code, even though it sounds like a law that couldn't possibly apply to more than half a dozen people. At least it has a catchy acronym—the ATLRSOC-NOCFWEVDHBMA Act.

The **White Phosphorus Matches Act** is plain enough, but it smacks of legislative timidity. Couldn't Congress deal with all colors of phosphorus matches in one fell swoop? And although estate lawyers swear that it is a valuable piece of legislation, the **Uniform Simultaneous Death Act** looks very much like the solution to a nonexistent problem:

> The Speaker: The House will now come to order! Do I hear a motion? The gentleman from Nebraska?
>
> Rep. Zilch: Mr. Speaker, we have got to do something about all these people dying simultaneously!
>
> Rep. Nonesuch: Let's pass a Simultaneous Death Act!
>
> Rep. Zilch: Yes—that's it! But for God's sake, let's make it *uniform*.

THE
PARTY
OF THE
FIRST
PART

204

Perhaps the best in this category is the British classic, the **Deceased Wife's Sister's Marriage Act 1907**, which was followed fourteen years later by the **Deceased Brother's Widow's Marriage Act**. Both statutes legalize marriages that would otherwise be technically incestuous under a 1540 law that codified scriptural prohibitions.

Finally, there is the stubborn fact that "popularity" is tied to a particular time and place. Nobody today would think to call a law the Non-Intercourse Act, but it worked like a charm once upon a time. Likewise, it is difficult to believe that the **Anti-Beer Act** was once thought to be a vote-getter. But it was. Signed into law by President Harding in 1921, the Anti-Beer Act was heralded for closing one of the most notorious loopholes in the Volstead Act: the fact that doctors were allowed to prescribe any form of liquor for "medicinal purposes." Somewhat improbably, beer had become one of America's leading pharmaceuticals during the early days of Prohibition. The Anti-Beer Act put an end to that, or tried to.

Even today—notwithstanding the use of polls and focus groups—it is surprising how many politicians have a tin ear when it comes to official popular names. A New Jersey law to encourage employees to report misconduct in the workplace was given the distinctly nerdy title **Conscientious Employee Protection Act**. Fortunately, everyone who knows the law calls it the **Whistleblower Act**, which is not only more economical, but also less likely to conjure up images of a ninety-pound weakling guarding the petty cash box.

Congressional legislation fares no better. The **Healthy Meals for Healthy Americans Act** sounds like a scheme to withhold food from sick people. A law to regulate tobacco—crying out for something snappy like the "Clean Lungs Act"—is given the dreary moniker **Tobacco Control Act**. In 1975, when Congress sought to protect consumers who buy shoddy cars, they named the law after the sponsors, the **Magnuson-Moss Warranty Act**. Commentators had a better name for it: the **Lemon Law**, which is the universally recognized title for the statute, and for similar state laws.

Despite their best efforts, legislators cannot always dictate what names become truly popular. **Blue Laws**, for example, was never an official popular name, but is actually a term of derision for state laws that prohibit certain retail activities, like buying alcohol, on Sunday. The name derives from the eighteenth-century slang use of "blue" to denote those who observed strict moral codes; it is related to the pejorative "bluenose," which also refers to a puritanical person.

The British local tax law introduced by Margaret Thatcher's government in the 1980s was officially called the **Community Charge**. But that name vanished from sight, as the public referred to the law as the **Poll Tax**, after an infamous tax that was levied in medieval England. At times, you see, a popular name is actually a testament to a law's unpopularity.

HOW TO ACHIEVE IMMORTALITY WITHOUT REALLY TRYING

THE
PARTY
OF THE
FIRST
PART

206

With such pitfalls potentially lurking behind popular names, it's small wonder that lawmakers so often fall back on the strategy of naming statutes after people. As we saw earlier, the person in question is often the sponsor of the legislation (the Volstead Act) or someone just like him (the Sherman Act). Usually, it is a combination of the House and Senate sponsors; for example, the **Smoot-Hawley Tariff Act of 1930**. Actually, according to congressional protocol, it should have been Hawley-Smoot—Hawley, as the House sponsor, was supposed to come first in any tariff bill. Senator Smoot, however, was the more popular politician, and so the law is generally written with his name first. Which worked out well for Hawley in the long run, since the statute—which sought to help the struggling economy by effectively cutting off international trade—was arguably the thing that put the "great" into the Great Depression.

Many statute names honor the work of people other than the sponsor—the **Fannie Lou Hamer, Rosa Parks, Cesar Chavez and Coretta Scott King Voting Rights Reauthorization and Amendments Act of 2006**, to cite one lengthy example. In recent years, Congress has passed the **Amy Somers Volunteers at Food Banks Act**, which recognizes the late director of the Second Harvest food bank; the **Mickey Leland Food for Peace Act**, which commemorates a congressman who was killed in a plane crash while on a famine relief mission in Ethiopia; and the **Sonny Bono Copyright Term Extension Act**, which pays tribute to copyright law.

A growing trend in criminal law is to name a statute after a victim of the crime that the statute seeks to prevent. Take **Megan's Law**, a state statute that requires public notice whenever a convicted sex offender moves into a neighborhood. The law is named for Megan Kanka, a girl who was murdered at age seven by a convicted sex offender. In New York alone, the governor has signed **Christopher's Law**, **Jenna's Law**, **Elisa's Law**, and **Lee-Ann's Law**. There is even **Buster's Law**, an animal cruelty statute, named for a tabby cat killed on the mean streets of Schenectady.

At the federal level, Congress has outdone itself with the **AMBER Alert Act**. It is an important law, named for Amber Hagerman, a nine-year-old Texas girl who was tragically murdered. Here's the neat thing: The law's name is also a backronym, standing for **America's Missing— Broadcast Emergency Response Alert Act**.

One wouldn't think that a popular name would commemorate the *perpetrator* of a crime, but it does happen. The **Tokyo Rose Statutes**—laws that prohibit foreigners from owning more than 25 percent of a United States broadcaster—are named for a woman convicted of treason for broadcasting enemy propaganda during World War II.

In 1977, New York passed the **Son of Sam Law**, which requires that convicted criminals give all money earned from book, movie, or other media deals to their victims or the state. The law was prompted by the efforts of convicted serial killer David Berkowitz (the "Son of Sam") to sell his story to the highest bidder. Following New York's lead, some forty states enacted Son of Sam laws. In the end, however, all that work was for naught because the Supreme Court struck down the Son of Sam Law on First Amendment grounds. Which just goes to show that anything that can go wrong will go wrong—otherwise known as **Murphy's Law**.

THE
PARTY
OF THE
FIRST
PART

208

10

FUTURE IMPERFECT

Future: Read as "former" (Pasmore v. Huggins).

— STROUD'S DICTIONARY OF WORDS AND
PHRASES JUDICIALLY INTERPRETED

Dora Kent was eighty-three years old when she passed away, peacefully, in Riverside, California. Shortly after her death, and according to her very specific instructions, Ms. Kent's head was removed from her body and the rest of her corpse was prepared for cremation.

The cremation did not take place as scheduled because the California Department of Health Services (DHS) refused to issue a death certificate, without which no crematorium would take the body. The reason for DHS's refusal was that the State of California was not entirely convinced that Ms. Kent—she of the severed head—was legally dead.

Ms. Kent's head, you see, had been cryogenically frozen in the hope that her brain would be "reanimated" at some future time and inserted into another body—preferably a body cloned from her own DNA. Under the circumstances, the DHS declared itself to be "at a loss" to determine Ms. Kent's legal status. Certainly, "dead" had a certain air of finality that seemed inappropriate for a person merely awaiting reanimation. Perhaps, the DHS suggested to state authorities, California should create a new category of **suspended persons**.

It is often said that technology will change our lives. From the standpoint of legal language, it appears to be more efficient at changing our deaths. **Dead** and **death** are among the oldest words known to the law; they come from Old English by way of ancient Scandinavian roots. For centuries these concepts caused the law very little trouble. *Black's Law Dictionary* gives the classic definition of death as "the cessation of life; permanent cessation of all vital functions and signs."

Technology has been playing havoc with the legal definition of death in recent years. Medical science has endowed us with machines that can keep at least some vital functions going indefinitely, meaning that people on life support could never die under the traditional definition. As a result, most state laws now define death as "the irreversible cessation of brain functioning"—in other words, **brain death**. That definition does limit the state's ability to declare a person to be dead when he or she exhibits even the most primitive of brain functions—and those functions can be quite persistent.

Still, decapitation normally does the trick. Except, briefly, in California, which was poised to be the first state to redefine death for the freeze-dried era. The Dora Kent affair ended up in litigation, naturally, with the DHS pitted against Alcor, the company to which Ms. Kent had entrusted her remains. While that case dragged on, the local prosecutor began to suspect foul play in Ms. Kent's death and launched a murder investigation focused on Alcor employees.

At this point—with one state official alleging that Dora Kent had been murdered and another one denying that she was dead—Alcor was understandably getting somewhat frustrated. It was not until 1992, five years after Dora Kent's death, that a California appellate court ordered DHS to issue a death certificate. In the meantime, the murder investigation was quietly dropped and Alcor moved its base of operations. It is now located in Arizona, which everyone says is a good place to get a head in business.

ATTACK OF THE CLONES!

Cryonics (the practice of freezing recently deceased people) may be a passing fad; or it may be the wave of the future. It's impossible to say at the moment. The only certainty is that it challenges traditional legal concepts such as death.

Some cryonics believers are putting property in trust for themselves so that when they are reanimated, there will be a nest egg, or even a house, waiting for them. As we saw in Chapter 7, however, the Rule against Perpetuities generally prevents people from tying up property longer than a life in being plus twenty-one years. Thus, a trust for a frozen person would almost certainly be void in many states, unless somehow one could convince a court that a person continues to be a "life in being" while he or she is suspended. But since that argument didn't fly in California's New Age courts, it seems unlikely to get far in Iowa.

Besides, even if you are successfully reanimated, whose identity would you assume? If legal death is meant to convey finality, then Dora Kent can never exist again. If her brain is brought back, who would she be? DHS posed this very question to the California appellate court; but the court refused to give an answer. When the time comes, the court assured DHS, the answer would be given.

A similar definitional conundrum lurks on the outskirts of **cloning**. At some point soon—or even now, depending on whom you believe—it may be possible to replicate yourself many times over. How should the law classify these mini-yous? Are they your children? Your siblings? You? According to one lobbying group, since a cloned human is "manufactured," it should be classified as

THE
PARTY
OF THE
FIRST
PART

212

personal property, leaving us with the arresting possibility that clones might someday be offered for sale, or perhaps *bequeathed* in the *testaments* of future Precision fiends (see Chapter 7).

Fifteen states have laws relating to cloning. California's was passed in 1997, but most of the other states' laws were enacted in the wake of the 2002 claim by a South Korean company called Clonaid to have produced the first human clone—a claim that was never substantiated. All the states to address the issue have banned **reproductive cloning** (cloning to produce another living being), or at least prohibited the use of public funds for that purpose; but some states allow **therapeutic cloning** (cloning of stem cells only).

The language of state cloning laws reads like nothing so much as a high school biology textbook. Rhode Island, for example, prohibits artificially dividing "a **blastocyst** [or] **zygote**"—words that state legislators rarely get the opportunity to bandy about. The Virginia statute forbids the transfer of a cell nucleus into an **oocyte**—only later explaining that *oocyte* "means the ovum or egg." Of course, the legislature could have just used ovum or egg in the first place, but by using oocyte they clearly signaled their intention to dominate the state Scrabble competition.

Virginia also bars the implantation of a cloned cell into a **uterine environment**. That may sound like a needlessly wordy way of referring to the uterus, but in this case the legislature may be justified in its inflated language. The creation of an artificial uterus may be just around the corner—researchers at Cornell University reportedly came close to developing one in 2002. The term "uterine environment" (the Massachusetts cloning law refers to a **uterine-like environment**) is broad enough to cover all uteri, real or artificial. It also gives sex maniacs a rare opportunity to describe themselves legally as "environmentalists."

THE FINAL FRONTIER

Clonaid—the company that caused the cloning scare—is controlled by the Raelian sect, whose members believe that the human race was created by extraterrestrials who cloned themselves and then, mysteriously, left us (the clones) to our own devices. Just in case the Raelians are right—and one likes to keep an open mind on such matters—it is comforting to know that legal language is ready for the day when our long-lost cousins come back for a family reunion.

Metalaw is the branch of law governing the relations between humans and other intelligent races. The field was launched by the late Andrew G. Haley in 1956, at a time when movies like *Invasion of the Body Snatchers* and *The Man from Planet X* fueled the popular feeling that flying saucers could land at any moment. Its founding principle is called the **Great Rule**: "Do unto others as they would have you do unto them"—which is the traditional "Golden Rule" rewritten to accommodate the fact that aliens may have different preferences from humans.

For the most part, metalaw is a theoretical exercise, but the United States did enact an **Extra-terrestrial Exposure Law** in 1969. UFO enthusiasts charged that the purpose of the law was—like the high barbed wire around the Roswell site—to keep ordinary citizens from contacting aliens. In fact, it was nothing more than an administrative regulation giving NASA the right to force returning

THE
PARTY
OF THE
FIRST
PART

214

astronauts to undergo a quarantine period. The law does at least provide a handy definition of **extra-terrestrially exposed**:

> . . . the state of condition of any person, property, animal or other form of life or matter whatever, who or which has:
>
> (1) Touched directly or come within the atmospheric envelope or any other celestial body; or
>
> (2) Touched directly or been in close proximity to (or been exposed indirectly to) any person, property, animal or other form of life or matter who or which has been extra-terrestrially exposed by virtue of paragraph (b)(1) of this section.

The regulation even provides a hypothetical illustration of what persons might be forced into quarantine: "if person or thing 'A' touches the surface of the Moon, and on 'A's' return to Earth, 'B' touches 'A' and, subsequently, 'C' touches 'B,' all of these—'A' through 'C' inclusive—would be extra-terrestrially exposed." Which is why, before shaking hands with a stranger, it always pays to ask "Have you been away from Earth lately?"

Metalaw is an offshoot of the much larger discipline known as **space law**, which deals with human activities in outer space. Most issues in space law fall under the jurisdiction of the United Nations. The rest is controlled by the Klingon Empire. Just kidding—actually, the rest of space law is a hodgepodge of bilateral agreements, national laws, and "norms" of questionable weight.

Space law is an exciting field for the legal linguist because the meanings of many of its key terms are still being worked out. **Space**, for example. Despite fifty years of conferences and summit meetings, space lawyers have yet to reach consensus on the legal definition of space. At some point *up there,* earth ends and space begins. But where does the earth end? Our atmosphere peters out after about eighty kilometers; low earth orbit is possible at one hundred kilometers; the earth's gravitational pull extends about thirteen million miles. So really, it's anybody's guess.

Yet the definition of space matters for a number of reasons. First, because a country retains jurisdiction over its adjacent airspace right up to the boundary with "space." In the 1976 Bogotá Declaration, a number of developing countries asserted that their national sovereignty extends all the way up to **geostationary orbit**, or about forty thousand kilometers straight up. This is a particularly valuable piece of cosmic real estate because it is where our communications satellites make themselves at home.

The definition of space also has serious implications for tort law. Liability for accidents involving spacecraft, which go by the legal name of **space objects**, is governed by the **Convention on International Liability for Damage Caused by Space Objects** (a **convention** is a form of international treaty—not to be confused with a gathering of sales reps at a local conference center).

In any event, the Liability Convention provides that if a space object collides with an aircraft, the country that launched the space object faces **absolute liability**, but if a space object collides with another space object, it's **fault liability**. The problem is that the Convention does not

THE
PARTY
OF THE
FIRST
PART

216

define "space object"; so the only way to distinguish a space object from an aircraft is that the former is intended to operate in space. Which brings us back to the definition of "space." Despite the unsettled nature of the law, one likes to imagine that a midspace collision would be handled amicably, with the astronauts exchanging insurance information, raising a glass of Tang, and zooming off to their favorite asteroids.

Speaking of which, another ubiquitous term in space law is **celestial bodies**—recall its use in the Extraterrestrial Exposure Law. The **Outer Space Treaty of 1967** prohibits "national appropriation" of the moon "and other celestial bodies." Everyone knows what the moon is, so the scope of the Outer Space Treaty depends on what is meant by "celestial bodies." Unfortunately, that term, like "space," is nowhere defined. The only thing one can say for certain about "celestial bodies" is that it sounds like a bit of cheesy copy from a *Sports Illustrated* swimsuit issue.

One could be forgiven for thinking that space lawyers purposely set themselves up for eternal definitional squabbles. At first, the consensus was that celestial bodies should refer to all planets, natural satellites of planets, and asteroids anywhere in the universe. More recently, space lawyers have tended to limit the term to those bodies found within our solar system—evidently they have enough on their plates without having to assume jurisdiction over Alpha Nebulon IV. There are even scholars who urge that "celestial bodies" must exclude any planet that is inhabited by intelligent beings. If there are intelligent aliens, the argument goes, they wouldn't be subject to the 1967 treaty; instead, they'd be covered by—you guessed it—metalaw.

The big losers in all these debates, by the way, are comets and meteoroids, which do not count as celestial bodies under anybody's definition.

2BR RNCH W/EARTH VU'S

You may have noticed that the Outer Space Treaty forbids "national appropriation" of celestial bodies. It does not say anything about individuals or corporations. That fact was not lost on a number of entrepreneurs, including an American named Dennis Hope, who in 1980 filed papers with the United States government and the United Nations laying claim to the moon and all the other planets of the solar system. He now runs a thriving business selling choice acreage on the moon and Mars to thousands of customers who may charitably be described as optimistic.

THE
PARTY
OF THE
FIRST
PART

218

Even before Hope staked his claim to the solar system, the U.N. Committee on the Peaceful Uses of Outer Space was working to preempt exploitation of celestial bodies. In 1979, the Committee proposed a new treaty—known as the **Moon Treaty**—declaring that the moon and the planets of the solar system are the "**common heritage of mankind**."

"Common heritage of mankind" may sound innocuous enough, but it is an extremely controversial phrase. It is taken from the **Law of the Sea Treaty** (1982), and the upshot of it is not only that nobody does own the planets, but that nobody *can* own them. That's a lot of property to turn your back on. While it is only speculation, the potential for lucrative mining operations on the moon, Mars, and various asteroids may have something to do with the United States and Russia's refusal to ratify the Moon

Treaty. In fact, as of this writing, only a handful of countries have ratified the Moon Treaty, none of which has a serious space program.

CYBERSPEAK

With the exception of those planning to develop summer cottages near the Sea of Tranquillity, most people living today are unlikely ever to encounter legal problems in outer space. Cyberspace, however, is another matter altogether.

In 2006, California courts considered the question of whether a blogger meets the legal definition of a **journalist**. The answer to the question has immediate consequences: If bloggers are journalists, then they can take advantage of **reporter's shield laws**—these are laws that give journalists the right to refuse to disclose information and confidential sources that they obtain in the course of their research. The trial court refused to grant journalist status to bloggers, but a California appellate court overruled that decision, giving bloggers the coveted status.

The blogger/journalist question is a typical issue in the growing field of **cyberlaw**, that is, the laws relating to computers, software, databases, networks, and, especially, the Internet. The "cyber" part comes from cybernetics (from the Greek *kybernetes,* a steersman or pilot), which is the study of communication and control among animals and machines.

Over the past decade, the cyber- prefix has been proliferating with depressing regularity throughout the legal vocabulary. Every law professor, it seems, imagines that by sticking "cyber-" in front of a traditional legal word, he or she will shoot to the top of the academy as though boosted by a Buck Rogers jetpack. Cyber really conveys very little, except that there might be some computer angle to the topic at hand. And it is the rare legal subject that cannot in some fashion be linked to a computer.

Today's law dictionaries just love to show that they are on top of this whole cyber thing. Look under *C* and you'll find definitions for **cybertorts**, **cyberfraud**, and **cyberattacks** (intriguingly, these are torts, frauds, and attacks committed via computer). You'll see **cybercriminals** in current dictionaries and, much to one's relief, **cybercops** to hunt them down.

THE
PARTY
OF THE
FIRST
PART

220

Cybersquatting is a novel form of cybertort. It involves the practice of registering an Internet domain name identical or similar to another person's trademark. The idea is that the trademark owner will pay up to get the squatter to release the domain name. A person who perpetrates such a scam is known as a cybersquatter or, more picturesquely, a **cyberpirate**. Under the **Anticybersquatting Consumer Protection Act of 1999**, trademark owners can sue cyberpirates or, presumably, make them walk the cyberplank.

Predators who use chat rooms and e-mail to target their victims may be guilty of **cyberstalking**. Those who use computer systems and networks to undermine national security risk prosecution for **cyberterrorism**.

There are jurists who wish to turn cyberlaw into a formal system of international law to govern the Internet. Some refer to this proposed system as **cyberalty**, a combination of cyber and **admiralty**—the latter because cyberspace is analogous to the high seas in that it is used by people of all nations. And because it's full of pirates.

VISIONS OF FUTURE PAST

It all sounds futuristic—or does it? To many, terms like "cyberlaw" and its derivatives are already passé, reminiscent of sci-fi chestnuts like cyborg and cybernaut. One alternative to *cyber-* is the prefix *e-*, as in **e-law**. This usage is sufficiently widespread to have been blessed by the *New York Times* in a 2002 headline that breathlessly announced "Libel Suit May Establish E-Jurisdiction." Granted, *e-* takes up less space than *cyber-,* but it looks just as silly. Sillier, actually.

A number of legal academics have suggested that **information law** is the most fitting name for the law related to computer networks. Still others reject both cyberlaw and information law as sounding too stodgy. Instead, they advocate a revolutionary terminology that transcends the limits of contemporary English vocabulary, a terminology that captures all the cutting-edge drama of the 'Net. I refer to Latin.

Yes, Latin. According to some experts, the international legal principles covering electronic exchanges of information ought to be known as **Lex Informatica**. *Lex* is Latin for law, and *Informatica* is Latin for—well, actually, it isn't Latin at all, but rather a pseudo-Latin word meaning "of or pertaining to information." *Lex Informatica* takes its inspiration from **Lex Mercatoria** ("Mercantile Law"), an ancient body of laws that governed the activities of merchants who traveled from one kingdom to another during the Middle Ages.

The use of Latin does have one great advantage: Since it is already a dead language, it can't get any deader. Technology lingo rapidly grows obsolete, and so do the corresponding legal terms. What we now call space law, for

FUTURE IMPERFECT

example, was in the late 1950s given the Jetsons-style label **cosmic law**. In 1960, a *Time* magazine writer urged government lawyers to pay attention to "**jet age** problems that cry for solution." In 1963, a California lawyer noted that various legal terms will take on a new meaning in the "**atomic age**." Perhaps someday cyberlaw and e-law will sound just as dated as those phrases while *Lex Informatica* remains relatively fresh, thanks to the embalming influence of Latin.

In the meantime, various high-tech legal problems are enriching our vocabulary every day. Perhaps the best-known affliction of the Internet era is spam, a term that is now defined by federal law. Under the 2003 CAN-SPAM Act (the name of which we admired so much in Chapter 9), spam is any unsolicited e-mail the "primary purpose of which" is to promote a commercial venture.

In any event, the CAN-SPAM Act makes it a misdemeanor to send spam with falsified "header" information: say, e-mails pretending to come from a prominent Nigerian barrister. Aggravated spamming under the Act includes such practices as **harvesting** e-mail addresses, **dictionary attacks** (a method for guessing passwords), and assaults by **Trojan horses** (malicious programs disguised as legitimate software).

Another way to attack a computer network is **smurfing**, which involves using a program that causes the target network to be flooded with so many requests that it becomes unavailable for legitimate traffic. Oddly enough, "smurfing" is also a recognized term to describe a type of money laundering. Hard to believe that a word made up by a Belgian cartoonist in 1959 is today used to describe two distinct offenses on the law books, but it's true.

THE
PARTY
OF THE
FIRST
PART

222

Throttling, another legal neologism, was the basis for a recent lawsuit against Netflix, a service that allows subscribers to order DVDs online. Allegedly, Netflix rationed the supply of popular DVDs by applying an undisclosed "fairness algorithm" that gave priority to new users and infrequent users. The fairness algorithm meant that regular Netflix customers sometimes faced delays of up to six days for popular titles, leading to widespread discontent— algorithm and blues, if you will.

A common problem for e-commerce merchants is **click fraud**, which is the illicit manipulation of keyword-based advertising. Click fraud can take many forms; one example would be a company employing people to click on a rival company's search engine ads, thereby driving up the competitor's advertising costs. But round-the-clock clicking is tedious work, so some click fraudsters, as well as many spammers, now do their deeds via **botnets**, that is, "robot networks." "Robot," incidentally, is a word invented by the Czech writer Karel Čapek in his futuristic play *Rossum's Universal Robots*. Čapek derived the word from *robota*, which in literary Czech refers to labor or drudgery.

DANGER, WILL ROBINSON

The very mention of robots conjures up images of the walking, talking, and vaguely sinister creatures that populate so many science fiction movies. Given advances in artificial intelligence and robotics, however, the reality is creeping up on fiction. Some scientists predict that we are not far from the day when robots will possess the kind of self-awareness and moral judgment that will make them more than mere machines.

Already computers can be programmed to compose po-etry. Will they someday demand copyright protection for their works? In Japan, some companies pay union dues for robots on the factory floor. What if the robots assert their right to strike?

Not surprisingly, legal scholars are already beginning to consider the possibility of **robot rights**. In 2004, the In-ternational Bar Association staged a mock trial in which a superintelligent computer sought to enjoin its "employer" from dismantling it. A 2006 report commissioned by the British government estimates that by the middle of the century, intelligent robots will start demanding rights, including **robo-healthcare**. One writer has suggested, only half jokingly, that there should be a crime of **roboslaugh-ter** for the unjustified destruction of a robot. Excellent. Now, would anybody care to grapple with a real-life legal problem?

Perhaps the more pressing issue is not what rights we will grant to machines, but what rights the machines will grant to us. In a 2001 interview, Stephen Hawking (no slouch, in my opinion) warned that "the danger is real that [computers] could develop intelligence and take over the world." Egads!

Ray Kurzweil, one of the pioneers of artificial intelli-gence, predicts a more complex future in which the hu-man and machine worlds become inextricably linked. Not only will humans receive increasingly sophisticated im-plants, but it may be possible someday to download the contents of a human brain onto a computer. Who knows? Dora Kent could end up inside somebody's hard drive. The future is a very strange place.

In Kurzweil's view, those who are more machine than human will eventually be calling the shots. Happily, Kurzweil predicts that the man-robots of the future will be inclined to grant rights to the **MOSH** (Mostly Original Substrate Humans)—that is, those who choose not to be "enhanced."

If any of this comes to pass, the law will need to develop a vocabulary to govern the relations among all the various gradations of man and machine. Kurzweil and his colleagues suggest that the law must broaden the meaning of **personhood** to include intelligent machines. Instead of "human rights," he argues, there should be a declaration of **sentience freedom**. Rabbi Norman Lamm, the chancellor of Yeshiva University, echoes these sentiments: "If a creature is both sentient and intelligent, and has a moral sense, then that creature should be considered a human being irrespective of the genesis of that person." In other words, computers are people too.

So we end up exactly where we began in Chapter 1: what does the law consider to be a **person**? A dog? A chimp? A robot? It's just one little word, person, but in the law a single word can reverberate with centuries' worth of meaning. To label someone, or something, a "person" is to endow that creature with a complex web of rights and responsibilities. Like other legal terms, person is not a word to be taken lightly.

The well-known rigidity of lawyers means that their vocabulary will almost certainly lag many years behind the scientific realities that are rapidly, unnervingly, reshaping our lives. On the other hand, a much underappreciated quality of lawyers—caution—suggests that legal language will be developed with some care. The law won't adopt new words (*Roboslaughter!*) just because they sound nifty. And that is reason enough to hope.

ONE MORE THING

What does the future hold for Plain English—will it prevail in its epic struggle against the Precision School?

It's still too early to tell, is the honest, if unsatisfying, answer. What *can* be said is that legal language is going through its most exciting period in many centuries. All across the English-speaking world, movements are afoot to make legalese more accessible to the general public. In Australia, the Centre for Plain Legal Language teaches lawyers in both public and private sectors the principles of plain English drafting. In the United States, consumer contracts and jury instructions are slowly but surely being rewritten in clean, modern prose. In the United Kingdom, the Plain English Campaign has won many victories, including the banishment of Latin from most court proceedings.

Even more encouraging is the fact that **plain language** and **plain English** have become "brands" in their own right. A database search of bills currently pending in the U.S. Congress turns up fifty-five bills containing the words "plain language." One of these bills, H.R. 4809, would require each government agency to follow the principles of plain language and to designate a **plain language coordinator** to ensure that the agency follows through.

And yet, plain English faces serious challenges. For one thing, it has to contend with the mindless cutting-and-pasting of outdated forms that are so easily stored on computers or downloaded from the Internet—**cyberlegalese**, if

THE
PARTY
OF THE
FIRST
PART

226

you will. Lawyers have to find the time, and the courage, to do without the security blanket of boilerplate and instead write documents that their clients will understand.

The culture of government and other large institutions still leans heavily toward stilted bureaucratic language because that sort of writing is perceived as safe. British officials face the additional challenge of **Euro-English**, that is, the English version of the European Union's pronouncements. This language combines the worst of English officialese with the unfamiliar constructions of other European languages. In Euro-English,

- A tax on production becomes a **co-responsibility levy**;
- A cow becomes an **adult bovine animal**;
- Lamb becomes **sheepmeat** (yum!).

In 2006, a group of French lawyers and academics launched a campaign to make French the official "legal language" of the European Union. Good. Let them have it.

Finally, plain language faces a barrage of criticism from a new generation of academics who do not necessarily defend traditional legal writing; they just don't believe in plain English. It's not clear how they think legal concepts are best conveyed. Semaphore, probably.

Robyn Penman of the Communication Research Institute of Australia summarized the new critique in her 1993 article "Unspeakable Acts and Other Deeds: A Critique of Plain Legal Language." In the first place, Penman argues, there is no "hard evidence" that plain language improves comprehension. That, of course, assumes that common sense is not hard evidence. She also asserts that plain language will not reduce litigation because lawyers will always quibble over words, plain or otherwise. *But if that's true,* one screams, mentally grabbing the nearest professor by the lapels, *what harm could possibly come from using plain language?*

One of the most persistent myths about plain language—the objection you'll hear over and over—is that it involves a simplistic see-Spot-run type of English that is unsuited to the legal problems of a complex world. It is difficult to know what to say to someone who has not grasped the distinction between simple and plain. Look in the dictionary would be my first suggestion.

Or consider the views of legal scholars Peter Butt and Richard Castle in their textbook *Modern Legal Drafting:* "Modern plain English is as capable of precision as traditional legal English. It can cope with all the concepts and complexities of the law and legal processes."

Or take a look at the first legal document created in the United States—the very document that brought the United States into existence. There you will find lucid prose:

> We hold these truths to be self-evident, that all men are created equal, that they are endowed by their Creator with certain unalienable Rights . . .

Those are not simple concepts; in fact, much of American history has been spent sorting out the meaning of those words. But you don't need a law degree to understand them; the language is plain, quite beautifully so.

Legal language belongs to everyone. Whether or not you are a lawyer, your life is bounded by legal formalities.

THE
PARTY
OF THE
FIRST
PART

228

Every day, you enter into agreements, sign waivers, renew leases, accept disclosures, and do a hundred other things that bring you into contact with legalese. But now you know something that most people don't: There is absolutely no law that *requires* anybody to use terms like **null and void, fit and proper, give, devise, and bequeath**, **aforesaid, herein, whereas**, or anything in Latin—ever.

There is, however, one Latin expression that is worth remembering: *Ignorantia juris non excusat* (Ignorance of the law does not excuse). Because of this principle, it is no defense in a criminal case to argue that you didn't realize that what you were doing was illegal. Likewise, it generally does you no good in a civil case to claim that you didn't understand the contract you were signing. Our very system of justice depends on the average citizen's ability to understand the law and legal documents. As a British judge wrote in 1985, "A society whose regulations are incomprehensible lives with the Rule of Lottery, not of Law."

The problem with traditional legalese is that it leaves most citizens in a state of, well, *ignorantia*. That's not because lawyers are evil. The vast majority of lawyers—even Precision-minded lawyers—are highly literate folk who wish to communicate clearly. As more and more lawyers learn the value of plain English, legal language will begin to regain the elegance and immediacy that is its birthright. With enough help, *legalese* could even become the ultimate accolade. Why not? Why not, indeed.

SELECT BIBLIOGRAPHY

LAW DICTIONARIES AND REFERENCE WORKS

Black, Henry Campbell, et al. *Black's Law Dictionary.* 6th ed. St. Paul: West Publishing, 1991.

Cowell, John. *The Interpreter.* Cambridge: John Legate, 1607. Reprinted by the Lawbook Exchange, Union, New Jersey, 2002.

Clapp, James. *Random House Webster's Dictionary of the Law.* New York: Random House, 2002.

Curzon, Leslie Basil. *Dictionary of Law.* 3rd ed. London: Pitman, 1983.

Renstrom, Peter G. *The American Law Dictionary.* Santa Barbara: ABC-CLIO, 1991.

Shumaker, Walter, and George Foster Longsdorf. *The Cyclopedic Law Dictionary.* Chicago: Callaghan and Co., 1922.

Stroud, Frederick. *Words and Phrases Judicially Interpreted.* London: Sweet and Maxwell, 1890. Reprinted by the Lawbook Exchange, Union, New Jersey, 2005.

West Group. *Words and Phrases.* 46 volumes. Permanent ed. (annually updated). St. Paul: West Publishing, 1940–present.

LEGAL LANGUAGE

Butt, Peter, and Richard Castle, *Modern Legal Drafting.* Cambridge: Cambridge University Press, 2001.

Garner, Bryan A. *The Elements of Legal Style.* 2nd ed. New York: Oxford University Press, 2002.

Duckworth, Mark, and Arthur Spyrou, eds. *Law Words: 30 Essays on Legal Words & Phrases*. Sydney: Centre for Plain Legal Language, 1995.

Gowers, Sir Ernest. *The Complete Plain Words*. Rev. ed. Boston: David R. Godine, 1986.

Kimble, Joseph. *Lifting the Fog of Legalese*. Durham: Carolina Academic Press, 2006.

Mellinkoff, David. *The Language of the Law*. Boston: Little, Brown & Co., 1963.

Plain English Campaign. *Language on Trial*. London: Robson Books, 1996.

―――. *Utter Drivel!* London: Robson Books, 1994.

Tiersma, Peter. *Legal Language*. Chicago: University of Chicago Press, 1999.

THE
PARTY
OF THE
FIRST
PART

232

LEGAL HISTORY AND TRIVIA

Baker, J. H. *An Introduction to English Legal History*. 2nd ed. London: Butterworths, 1979.

Barnett, Walter. *Sexual Freedom and the Constitution*. Albuquerque: University of New Mexico Press, 1973.

Blackstone, Sir William. *Commentaries on the Laws of England*. 4 volumes. 1765–69.

Chapin, Bradley. *Criminal Justice in Colonial America, 1606–1660*. Athens, Georgia: University of Georgia Press, 1983.

Friedman, Lawrence M. *A History of American Law*. 2nd ed. New York: Simon & Schuster, 1985.

Megarry, Sir Robert. *Miscellany-at-Law*. London: Stevens & Sons, 1955.

―――. *A Second Miscellany-at-Law*. London: Sweet & Maxwell, 1973.

―――. *A New Miscellany-at-Law*. Oxford: Hart Publishing, 2005.

ACKNOWLEDGMENTS

I probably would not have developed this strange obsession with legalese had the folks at New York Law Journal Magazine not invited me to write a column called "Legal Lingo" back in 2002. I am grateful to editors Rex Bossert, Charles Carter, Anthony Paonita, Michael Paquette, and Jeff Storey for their help and encouragement over the years. I must also acknowledge my debt to writers such as Peter Tiersma, Bryan Garner, Joseph Kimble, and the late David Mellinkoff for blazing the trail along which I now slouch.

In writing this book, I received invaluable support and assistance from my parents and siblings, as well as from friends Bart Aronson, Sheri Berman, John Canoni, Gerald Fradin, Charlotte and Barry Kingham, Rob Long, Lauren Osborne, Gideon Rose, and Paula and Fareed Zakaria. Linda Holmes at Brooklyn Law School graciously allowed me to use that school's excellent library. At Henry Holt, my editor, Sarah Knight, devoted extraordinary time and energy to matters of style and substance—many thanks to her and her highly professional assistant, Patrick Clark, as well as to production editor Devin

Coats and copy editor Emily DeHuff. My agent and steadfast ally, Geri Thoma, is simply the best.

Finally, this book could not have been written without the inspiration and support provided by my wife, Kathleen, every step of the way. To her, this book is dedicated.

THE
PARTY
OF THE
FIRST
PART

234

INDEX

punctuation, criminal law and placement of, 118–20

ABOUT THE AUTHOR

ADAM FREEDMAN has written the "Legal Lingo" column for the *New York Law Journal Magazine* since 2002 and was a litigator in New York City before joining a major investment bank, where he currently earns his living decoding policies and procedures into plain English. He holds degrees from Yale, Oxford, and the University of Chicago and has written for *Newsweek International,* Slate.com, and the *Guardian Weekly,* among others. He lives in Brooklyn, New York.